SOLSTICE

a winter anthology
[volume 2]

DEVIL'S PARTY PRESS | LOS ANGELES

SOLSTICE
a winter anthology
[volume 2]

Dianne Pearce, Editor and Publisher.
Designed by David Yurkovich.

ISBN: 978-1-957224-03-9

devilspartypress.com

CONTENTS

SOLSTICE

INTRODUCTION

The winter solstice occurs in December in my part of the world, though in the Southern Hemisphere it takes place in June. It marks the day when the sun is in the sky for the shortest amount of time. For us in the Northern Hemisphere, especially, I would venture to say, in the United States, it occurs during a time of extreme busyness, because it happens right around Christmas, Hannukah, Kwanzaa, the New Year celebrations.

While some people draw great strength from lots of activity with others, I'm really an introvert, and I think the winter solstice is really meant for a bit of introversion, and introspection, for us all. There is a sense I have that if we're all running around trying to have fun, buy the perfect gift, throw or attend the perfect party, well, we're doing it all wrong. Like a bear, we should be going indoors, not answering the phone (the bears never seem to take my calls anyway, even in summer), snuggling up, and taking the pressure off. How are you going to make your News Year's resolution if you never give yourself a moment to reflect on the prior 365 days?

Our 2017 *Solstice* anthology was among the first books published by Devil's Party. We decided to produce a new volume because we really enjoy the exercise of a forced slowdown. I know the COVID-19 pandemic lockdown here in the United States during 2020 made everyone alter their daily lives, ready or not, and for many, that alone was difficult, to say nothing of the losses of loved ones many suffered during this time.

But all of our activities can easily turn into a treadmill, and sometimes it helps just to be pulled away from it. It can feel, at least with my East Coast city upbringing, lazy to not be a go-go-go person. And yet, for my family, the time and the space the lockdown created to really live with ourselves helped us to see that we needed to make changes—do more of some things, and less of others—for our own growth and well-being. It was as if we were forced to look back over our story so far and edit it rather than to just keep on the breakneck pace of writing it. I hope we never have to experience another lockdown, or the losses that necessitated it, but I also hope we have collectively learned to take a breath, to look behind, and within, and figure out whether we're on the path that heads to where we want to be.

In this volume of stories and poems you will encounter nature, loss, renewal, food (if you're gonna hibernate, you gotta eat), sleep, bitter cold, and surprising warmth. Some of the authors have been writing for decades, and some are publishing their first piece here, just getting going on their second act. Each of their works has moved me in a way that made it impossible not to select them.

I want to suggest that, as you read this lovely volume, you also read the bios, and then search the authors online to see if you can find more of their work. I can recommend them as the perfect authors to hibernate with, and it's our mission to promote the beautiful complexity that people of a certain age bring to their writing. Each story and poem you read here represents someone's gift to you, but also someone's dream, and you can stretch their dream just a little further when you find, read, and support other works they've written. This book is a gift to you, and you can be a gift to the authors in return. Writing is an exchange. If any of the works in this collection move you, I'm certain the authors would love to hear about it.

I want to take a moment to discuss the cover. In December 2009, on the winter solstice, my husband and I finally met and held our daughter in China. It was bitter cold in Beijing the day before, when we, on our last day childless, out wandering around the cold, snowy city, and getting by on my limited Mandarin, had a group of college art students stop to try and help us to find Mao's tomb. We never did find Mao, but instead discovered something far more interesting as we were taken to their school's art show, where we were delighted to purchase a few pieces of their marvelous work, among them this lovely painting. To us, it's a winter painting, and we love everything about it. This painting and the winter solstice will always be special to us for the warm hospitality we received from everyone we encountered during our stay in China, and for the best gift we ever received in our lives, a daughter, who also happens to be an artist. Maybe it was serendipity, and if it was, I want to say that it never would have happened had a bunch of students not reached out to help us, and had we had not been open to trusting individuals with whom we couldn't even converse. And maybe the solstice is about that too, hunkering down in some ways, and opening up in others.

I am glad you bought this book, because I know you're going to enjoy it, even the sad bits, even the lonely bits. All the bits are beautiful. And I am grateful for you, the reader these writers crave. Thank you for your friendship to them. I wish for you a wonderful solstice and New Year. May you enjoy some solitude and introversion. And when you're ready for some company, may you meet with a friend to share both a warming drink, and your copy of this lovely book.

Dianne Pearce (she/her/hers)
December 2022
Los Angeles

the breath of winter

Morgan Golladay

I become enchanted
with the breath of winter.

Palpable,
ethereal,
transient,
life made visible.

Its taste is upon my lips,
hinting at a newness of life.
It only lingers a moment,
leaving me longing for spring.

Tinsel

Lisa Short

Zenia had chosen the place, an Applebee's—it had been her favorite restaurant when she was little, or at least that's what her mother had told me the handful of times we'd met there for lunch. I wondered if she'd chosen it on purpose, but found it hard to imagine her putting even as much effort as that into our meeting today.

The holly-studded wreath above the door chimed merrily as I pushed the door open—they'd gone all-out at this particular location for the holidays. Tiny Christmas trees lurked in every corner and the hostess's station sparkled with red and green lights; Rudolph the Red-Nosed Reindeer belted out over the speakers. "Hi!" said the hostess cheerfully—she was about Zenia's age, in her late teens, and uncomplicatedly pretty. I caught sight of my reflection in the bar mirror behind her. Bacardi for the Holidays! the mirror proclaimed, over my own rather tired-looking features.

I spotted Zenia fairly quickly, though I hadn't seen her in at least five years—her hair was the same, though, waist-length and fine as gossamer, raw umber flecked with gold. The hostess nodded cheerfully when I told her I was meeting someone, following my gaze to where Zenia sat.

Zenia didn't look up as I approached; she sat stiffly, as motionless as the table bolted to the floor in front of her. I pulled out a chair and sat down opposite her.

"Hey," I said. "It's me—" I never knew what to call myself, to her. She had so seldom addressed me by anything in the nineteen years I'd known her. It seemed an unwanted intimacy to force a label of kinship on her now.

She did focus on me then, and as always I was taken aback by the beauty of her eyes. They were like her mother's but drawn by a fantasist instead of a portrait artist—larger, more crystalline, the lashes as long and delicate as spider threads. "Thanks for coming," she said, her tone light and empty. "I need money."

No small talk, then—I wasn't sure if I was relieved or disappointed, and if the latter, which of us I was disappointed in. "How much?" She could certainly ask for too much, more than my meager love for her would compel me to give her. I hoped she wouldn't.

"A thousand." She didn't bother to hide the calculation in her eyes, and why should she? I did try to hide the relief in mine by hunting for my wallet. "You brought a thousand with you?" There was enough genuine emotion in that to pull my attention back to her face— something lurked there, behind her fairy-glass eyes, though I couldn't begin to guess what.

"Yes," I said gently—I did love her enough for that. I handed her the money, a thick wad of twenties and fifties. She took it, then stood up abruptly. The full moon of her belly rose over the table, the slice of bare skin beneath her cropped t-shirt a roadmap of purple stretchmarks.

"Well," she said, staring past the top of my head. "Goodbye." I watched her walk away until she vanished from sight through the restaurant doors.

"Merry Christmas," I said, into the emptiness she left behind.

"Ma'am?" I started, but it was just the hostess. "Would you like anything to drink? Or do you want to wait for your daughter to come back?" She smiled brightly down at me. "My mom and I always get together for dinner and drinks over the holidays, it's like a family tradition!"

A family tradition—how horrible, so horrible it was almost funny. That very first Christmas, thirty-eight years ago, when I'd found myself shoved unceremoniously out the door, clutching my still-flat belly roiling with nausea, my mother's drunken shrieks muffled by the deep-piled snow all around our porch. And then another Christmas, nineteen years later—no drinking, no shouting, no shoving that time, but my daughter had left anyway, stomping through the snow to her boyfriend's waiting car, its great plumes of exhaust billowing up from the driveway into the cold night air.

"She's not my daughter," I said. "She's my granddaughter." The hostess's smile wobbled. I let it go, because I already had in every other way that mattered, and smiled reassuringly back up at her. "Sure. A Bacardi and Coke. And don't worry about waiting for her order. She's not coming back."

Heat

Jane Fitzgerald

My mother used to tell me
How her father would arise
Before the first light of dawn
Descending to the basement
To shovel coal into the furnace
Warming the old frigid house
While the family slept soundly above

When I was a child
My father, too, left his bed in darkness
To mechanically turn on the boiler
Causing the hot water to pump
Through the heavy iron radiators
The rushing and knocking noises
Would slowly wake me up
Allowing precious time to languish in bed
And feel the lovely warmth
Spread across my icy room
At night my clothing was set on the radiator
By morning the fabric felt like the sun
Gently touching my skin

I was shielded from the harsh reality
Of comfortless cold winter dawns
Not aware until I was an adult
How these acts of selflessness
Begun before the bone-chilling break of day
Left a corollary of sacrificing love
Passing on a pattern for generations to come

Shower

Jane Fitzgerald

On this glacial cold dawn
I'm taking a steamy hot shower
The warmth cascades over my body
Causing me to feel compassion
For those without this cleansing luxury
A common place act so many of us take for granted
I'm forever grateful for life's basic element
It refreshes my tired muscles and mind
Every pore in my being
Cries out appreciation and thankfulness
But is the comforting, purifying shower
Really enough when
The dirt and demons of the day
Await me

When I was a Child

Jane Fitzgerald

As far back as my young mind can envision
Our large eclectic extended family
Convened from Christmas through New Year's Day
At my grandparents' massively chilly Victorian house

Its vast gloominess was both scary and thrilling
There were eight bedrooms and two moon high staircases
The many passages were like shadowy rabbit warrens
Perfect avenues for hours of frenzied hide and seek

All of the grownups vehemently claimed
Their familiar heated comfortable bedrooms
The bigger kids grudgingly shared bunk beds
in a drafty room over the garage
Since I was the youngest of this riotous rabble
My sleeping arrangements consisted
of the frigid floor or couch

I soon discovered the best secret of all
My grandparents' room harbored a huge closet
It was located above the boiler in the basement
Behind their clothing was a deep warm recess
Reaching all the way back to the eerie slanting eaves
Providing lots of space for a clandestine chamber

I furtively dragged blankets, pillows and flashlight
Creating a special secret sanctuary
My torch transported me to far-away worlds
I suffered a spider bite with the Swiss Family Robinson
My heart broke when Black Beauty was beaten
I happily painted Tom Sawyer's fence

SOLSTICE

Long intriguing stories were penned in my journal
Giving me a second life with my imaginary friends
My precious portable radio kept me company
Actively chasing the bad guys with Hopalong Cassidy

This euphoric eccentric existence continued
Until I was nearing twelve years old when
My cozy closet felt the sharp winter wind
My aging grandparents reality shifted to purgatory
Unable to manage their beloved lifelong haven
They were inconsolably displaced to a retirement home
That Christmas the arctic descended over the old empty house

The Colorful Goodbye
Maggie Claypool

As the plane circled out over Lake Superior, Lee looked out at the Michigan coast. He didn't expect to see his family's cabin northwest of Marquette from that distance, but he knew that it was there somewhere in all that snow.

It had been five years since he'd last stepped foot in Michigan's Upper Peninsula, where he'd spent the best times of his childhood. In summertime, his family had spent long weekends and at least one full week up at the cabin—hiking, camping, fishing, swimming, canoeing. Lee, his parents and his two brothers were outdoors from sunup to well into the night. During autumn, the men spent a week bow hunting, while Lee's mom, Joann, made soup and chili. Winter was the time Lee loved the most. They'd get the "sleds"—what they called their snowmobiles—out of the shed and ride the trails. And there was ice fishing and snowshoeing, roaring fires, and lots of "Irish cocoa" as his dad called it—more "Irish" than cocoa.

Lee's memories of those winters were warm – in his mind, he could see his dad's face glowing from the fire and the whiskey as he laughed. Looking out at the ice pellets pinging off the plane, he felt nothing of that remembered warmth.

After deplaning, he grabbed his duffle bag from the luggage cart and headed inside to see about renting a car. When he stepped outside the secure section of the airport, however, he spied his brother, Sean, in the waiting area. Even in a parka and a stocking cap, there was no mistaking Sean's six-foot-five frame and bushy blonde beard.

Lee was immediately annoyed and made no attempt to hide it. He walked toward Sean, and when within speaking distance, he said coldly, "What are you doing here?"

"Good to see you, too," Sean responded. "I thought it would be a good idea if we had some time together before we're all at the cabin. Ben and his whole crew are already there."

"Yeah, well, I'm going to rent a car, so, thanks, but you can head back, and I'll see you there."

"Yeah, well, Sean said, mocking Lee's tone, "All they have left are two-wheel drives, and the roads outside of Powell are not cleared. So, unless, you want to spend time in a ditch …."

Sean's eyes did not waver from his as Lee stared at him appraisingly. Lee was pissed, but he figured Sean was telling the truth, and he knew he wouldn't get to the cabin without four-wheel drive. Grudgingly, he growled, "Okay, let's go," and followed Sean out to his truck.

As they drove north, Sean periodically pointed out sights that had changed since the last time Lee had been there. Lee acknowledged Sean's commentary with nothing more than grunts. The roads became increasingly more treacherous, and Sean's commentary ceased; they rode for the better part of an hour in silence.

When they turned onto the county road south of Powell, it was completely snow-covered. Several miles later, they turned onto an unpaved and uncleared secondary road; the snow was easily ten inches deep. Sean, having grown up in Michigan, confidently negotiated the road.

A couple miles from the cabin, Lee looked for the tree where he'd stuck his sled the winter he was thirteen. It was a huge, ancient pine, and he'd been cutting donuts around it as fast as he could. He'd kept trying to draw his circles tighter around the tree, missing his father's shouted warning. When his head had skimmed the underside of a limb drooping with snow, he'd whooped with sheer joy. Without warning, the machine had fallen out from under him into the tree well. His dad had pulled him out, made sure he wasn't badly hurt, and then went ballistic—Lee had never seen his dad so furious. He had assumed it was because he'd wrecked the sled, but his mom told him later it was because his dad had been so afraid he was seriously hurt.

Lee never bought that explanation until he had kids of his own. *Kids Dad hasn't seen in five years,* he thought. Immediately after that thought, he realized the pine tree was missing, and he turned to Sean in confusion. Before he even said anything, Sean said, "It started dying about four years ago, and Gruber cut it down the year before last. Conservation estimated it was four hundred years old." Sean chuckled.

"The old man was a bit off in his estimate." Their father had always said the giant pine was six hundred years old.

Looking out the window, Lee said nothing. The tree he'd always thought of as his tree was gone. He felt cold and alone, and he felt resentful—someone should've told him his tree was dying. That resentment settled with other aged grievances in the pit of his stomach.

In another few minutes, they pulled into the driveway.

Although the family referred to it as "the cabin," at this point, sixty plus years since the original five-room structure had been built, it had had grown to be more accurately described as a lodge. It was on the west side of a wooded mountain. From the front it looked like a two-story pine lodge, but the backside revealed a lower level that walked out onto a small deck, with a large, extended deck on the main floor that wrapped around the cabin's south side.

Lee got out of Sean's truck, and, still silent, carried his duffle bag over to the wide and welcoming front porch, but rather than entering the cabin's double doors, he turned left and strode to the back deck just as the sun sank below the thick, dark clouds that gave way to a brief expanse of bright sky on the western horizon. The brilliant rays illuminated that layer of clear sky, and shaded the bordering clouds breathtaking hues of coral and fuchsia that were reflected in the snow covering the ground in all directions. Lee said quietly, "There's your sunset, Mom."

A voice behind him said, "She did love the sunsets from back here." Lee whirled to find his youngest brother, Ben, seated behind him.

"You scared me!" Lee said. "How long have you been there?"

"Since before you came stomping back here."

"I wasn't stomping."

"You were stomping."

Lee couldn't help but smile back at his baby brother grinning at him..

Ben asked, "How was the ride up here with brother Sean?"

"Long," was all Lee said.

"Hmm," replied Ben.

"What the hell is that supposed to mean?" Lee demanded.

"Absolutely nothing," Ben said evenly. "I just didn't know what to say." Then he added, "I guess, though, that I'd hoped you and Sean would talk, and I think that's what Sean was hoping, too."

"Might as well just fart into the wind," Lee growled.

Ben threw his head back and laughed, "Damn, if you don't sound just like the old man!"

"Are you *trying* to piss me off?"

"Doesn't seem to take much trying." Ben fired back in his annoyingly even tone. Let's go inside—you have some nieces and nephews dying to get a look at you." With that, Ben got up from his chair and stepped to the door. Lee took a deep breath and followed him.

There was loud chatter going on inside, but when Lee stepped inside behind Ben, everyone went silent. He turned to close the door, exhaling forcefully from his mouth as he did so. When he turned back around, he had a weak smile on his face as he looked at his brothers, their wives, and their children.

"Look who I found out on the back deck!" Ben said in a loud, cheery voice, "your Uncle Lee!"

"Hi, everybody," Lee said much more quietly.

A little girl walked up to Lee, cocked her head to the side and said, "You do look just like Uncle Sean, but with brown hair! But, I thought you were s'posed to have a beard like his."

Lee fully smiled for the first time since he'd gotten up that morning and said, "You must be Bella. I shaved my beard when it turned gray 'cause it made me look like an old man." He tousled her hair, and then all the other kids rushed over to meet their mysterious uncle.

Sean leaned against the kitchen island while Evvie, his wife, walked right up to Lee and wrapped her arms around him. As she hugged him tight, she whispered, "I'm so glad you made the trip back." Lee lightly hugged her in return, and gave her a tight smile.

"Lee, you remember my wife, Jenna?" Ben asked with his arm around his petite wife.

Lee nodded at her, and she said, "Good to see you again. Amy called to make sure you made it. You might wanna give her a call before dinner, and I hope you like tacos."

Ben added, "You're in the corner bedroom downstairs."

Lee told the kids he'd be back up in a bit and went downstairs to the bedroom. He sat down on the bed and called his wife.

"Hello?" came Amy's sweet voice.

"It's me," Lee said.

"How's everything going?"

"The flight out of Detroit was delayed, and then we circled Marquette for half an hour. And then," Lee paused, "Sean showed up at the airport to pick me up."

Amy said slowly, "Okaaay, how'd that go?"

Lee mumbled, "I don't wanna talk about it." Then, more brightly, he said, "Tell me about your day."

They chatted for several minutes. Each time Amy tried to turn the conversation to Lee's family, he redirected her to other topics. But he wasn't really listening to her because he was too wrapped in the drama that was playing out in his head.

Finally, Amy said, "Okay, out with it."

Lee shot back, "What are you talking about?"

"I just told you that our twelve-year-old daughter skipped school, and you said, 'Mmm.'"

"She what?" Lee exclaimed.

"I was seeing if you were listening. You're not. Tell me what happened with Sean."

"It's fine."

"You think I don't know after sixteen years of marriage when something's not fine? Tell me what's wrong."

Lee paused and then bitterly laughed. "Well, not a damn thing with my so-called family has changed. I found out on the ride up here, that my tree..." his voice broke, "...my tree died, and nobody told me." In a choked voice he continued. "It's just like with Mom. They knew the tree was sick, and nobody reached out to tell me. They cut it down, and nobody told me about that either. I don't even know what I'm doing here. I'm going to get back to the airport in the morning and come home."

"Lee," Amy said. "As they say on TV, you're assuming facts not in evidence. Your dad and brothers have contacted you I don't know how many times over the past five years. You refuse to take their calls or read their messages. Ben had to track me down to let you know about your dad's accident. They may have tried to tell you about the tree."

Lee snapped, "So, you're saying it's my fault?"

"I'm not saying it's anybody's fault, Lee. All I'm saying is that you don't know that they didn't try to tell you. Honey, I think you need to be with your brothers this weekend. I'm afraid if you don't, you'll regret it later."

When Lee didn't respond, Amy continued, "Maybe talk with Ben about the tree tomorrow. See what he has to say."

"I'll think about it. I'm sorry I snapped at you, babe. I just don't know how I'm gonna get through dinner. It was at that table that Sean beat the shit out of me after we spread Mom's ashes."

Amy said dryly, "The way I remember it, you gave as good as you got."

"Well, he started it."

Amy was silent.

"I can hear you judging me," Lee said.

"No, you hear me trying to figure out how I can help you from here. All I can say, is take it easy tonight, and talk with Ben in the morning."

"Okay, I'll let you know how that goes."

After saying goodbye, Lee thought about five years before, when his dad told him that his mom was in the hospital and wasn't going to make it. He had immediately jumped on a plane and rushed to his mom's hospital room. He was unprepared for what he saw: his glowing, beautiful mother was a sallow bag of bones fading in and out of a morphine stupor.

Their conversation had been brief. They exchanged "I love yous," and his mom asked him to take care of his dad and brothers. Then she said she needed to rest. She closed her eyes and didn't wake again.

She had already made plans for her memorial. She'd planned to be cremated, and she wanted her husband and sons to release her ashes in the Huron Mountains on their wedding anniversary, January 22. She had died on January 15, and so the next week had been a flurry of activity to put her plans into action.

Lee's folks had always loved to take moonlit snowmobile rides to Thomas Rock Overlook, and so the family had decided to make the trek after sunset. After his dad, John, released his mother's ashes into the icy air, they'd gone back to the cabin, lit a bonfire, and drunk Irish cocoa. An hour in, none of the men bothered with the cocoa. Lee had voiced his astonishment that the cancer had come back with such a vengeance and took his mom so quickly. It was then that his dad had told him that the cancer had returned six months before, but his mom hadn't wanted to undergo chemo again, and hadn't wanted to tell anyone about the cancer or her decision. She'd wanted to live her last months on her terms.

Lee was dumbfounded and drunk. For several moments, he just kept pointing at his father and repeating, "What are you saying to me?" When he had found his words, he verbally eviscerated his father who, every bit as drunk as Lee, had sat and took it, the tears streaming down his face. Both brothers and Amy had tried to stop Lee, but he kept going until he fell to the ground. Then, he'd gotten up, gone inside, and started packing his family's bags. Amy had gone after him, and eventually she'd convinced him to stay the night.

The next morning, Lee had awakened at first light with a massive headache and had gone to the kitchen for coffee. Sean was seated at the long, wooden trestle table, and Lee had grunted at him as he walked past, poured himself the last of the coffee and brewed another pot. When Lee had brought his coffee to the table, Sean had said, "Well, I hope you're satisfied. Because of your bullshit last night, Dad left."

Lee had sat down and said, "Good. If I had to look at that son of a bitch this morning, I'd punch his face in."

Twice Sean had raised his hand and started to berate his brother, and twice he closed his mouth and lowered his hand in frustration. Then he'd gotten up from the bench and started to walk away. Suddenly, he'd whirled and caught Lee with a roundhouse, knocking him off the bench. The fight had been on then, and it had woken everyone else. When it was over, all the kids were crying and both men were bruised and bloody. Lee's last words to Sean had been that he never wanted to see him or their father, again. "Fine by me," Sean spat back.

Tonight, when Lee went upstairs, everyone was waiting for him. Ben yelled, "There he is! Let's get this taco line started!"

With that, they all filled their plates and gathered around the trestle table. The kids, enjoying being together and the novelty of a long-lost uncle, kept the evening lively, and Lee eventually relaxed and even enjoyed himself. After helping clean up after dinner, he announced that he was exhausted and bid everyone good night.

"Hold on a second," Ben said. "Here's what I'm thinking about for tomorrow. Breakfast is a fend-for-yourself kinda deal, then we all gather for lunch, say, noonish, and after lunch, I read Dad's will, and then, after we toast the sunset, we ride. Sound like a plan?"

Everyone responded that it did, indeed, sound like a plan, and Lee retired for the night. The next morning, he woke and quietly went upstairs. When he turned toward the kitchen, he saw Ben sitting at the kitchen island

"Mornin'," Ben said.

"Mornin'," Lee replied walking over to the coffee pot. "You're up pretty early."

"Wanted to make sure I had some time with you."

Lee, his back to Ben, said evenly. "Oh, yeah? Why's that?"

He heard Ben take a deep breath. "Because, you barely said ten words last night, and it's pretty clear to me that if everyone's around, I'm not gonna get a chance to find out how my big brother is doing."

Lee turned and leaned against the counter as he looked across the island at his brother. "I'm fine," he said.

"No, you're not," Ben shot back. "When you came rushing back on the deck yesterday, you looked like a man about to bawl."

"I was not bawling!" Lee exclaimed.

"I said, 'about to.' Good God, you're touchy!"

They faced each other in silence. Lee took a sip of coffee and said, "I have a question."

"Shoot."

"Why didn't anyone tell me about the pine tree in Grubers' meadow dying?"

"Well, I know Dad tried to tell you about it," Ben said. "And he spent a small fortune trying to save it."

"Wh-what?" Lee stammered.

"Yeah, when Conservation told him there was nothing that could be done, he brought in some arborist from California. They tried all sorts of shit, but none of it made any difference."

Lee considered that, but then said, "Somebody should've fuckin' told me! That tree was there for some of the biggest moments of my life, and nobody told me. Just like with Mom."

Ben shot back tersely, "It was nothing like Mom, and I already told you that Dad tried to get a hold of you." Then, he added, "And, the day they cut it down, Dad left you a message about how sorry he was."

After a moment of silence, Lee took another swallow of coffee and said dully, "My earliest memory is of Dad taking me there to pick up pinecones for Mom." Then a little more brightly, "When I was about five, I wanted to decorate it for Christmas, and Mom pulled out some old garland and ornaments, and she and I decorated the lowest branches. Dad showed up with a star, and he climbed the tree and wired the star to the top. Scared Mom to death."

Ben smiled as Lee continued, "Dad taught me and Sean to drive the snowmobiles right there in the meadow. Then the summer I was about eleven and Sean was nine, Gruber got some cigarettes, and we were trying to smoke out under the pine. Dad and Old Man Gruber caught us, and made us smoke every damn cigarette in that pack. We three boys ended up puking under the tree, with Dad and Old Man Gruber laughing their asses off!"

Both brothers laughed, and then Lee said, "Then there was the time I ran the sled into the tree well…"

Ben interjected, "Yeah, I remember that one!" Then, gently, he said, "It sounds to me like the tree is not the center of those memories. Mom and Dad are. I think that's why you're so upset about the tree."

Lee, surprised at Ben's words, looked at him a moment, shook his head and said, "I'm going snowshoeing."

After he strapped on the snowshoes, he stepped out of the shed, breathed in the fresh, cold air and watched his breath swirl around his face. He felt the familiar exhilaration he'd always felt being out on the mountain in winter, all cares temporarily forgotten in the crunching snow. He snowshoed for a couple of hours before returning to the cabin feeling calmer. He went downstairs to shower, and by the time he finished getting dressed, he heard everyone upstairs. He steeled himself and went up. The kids greeted him and excitedly told him about their morning adventures while Evvie and Jenna put out sandwich fixings.

After lunch, the brothers went downstairs to the family room for the reading of the will. They sat themselves on the overstuffed furniture—Ben on one sofa, with his laptop on the hewn wood coffee table, Lee on the opposing sofa, and Sean in an armchair.

Ben immediately donned his attorney persona and began the proceedings, which he recorded on his cellphone. John left each of his nine grandkids $15,000. He left the house in Grand Rapids and its contents to all three sons, with instructions that they come to mutual agreement on any personal mementos, sell everything else, and split the proceeds evenly. Then they came to the cabin.

John left the cabin and his remaining financial assets in a trust with all three sons named as beneficiaries. He named Ben as the administrator of the trust, with fiduciary responsibilities to his brothers. Then, Ben dropped the last instruction like a bomb: To remain beneficiaries of the trust, all three brothers had to spend a week together at the cabin each year. If any brother failed to do so, he would receive $50,000 and be removed from the trust. If all three brothers declined this provision, all assets in the trust would go to the Michigan

Land Conservancy. If the brothers met the conditions of the trust for fifteen years following John's death, they could decide whether to dissolve the trust equally, or renew it.

Lee exclaimed, "So, he thinks he's going to control me from the grave?" Ben raised a hand, but Lee just barreled on. "Fuck that," he said. "I'm out, and you can keep the $50,000. I don't want a penny of his…manipulation money."

Sean's face turned red, but he kept silent as Ben withdrew a white envelope from his computer bag. He offered it to Lee and said, "I'd suggest you read this before you decide anything."

On the envelope was Lee's name in his father's elegant script. Lee looked at Ben and said, "What's this?"

"I don't know. Whatever it is, it's meant for you alone."

Lee, seeing Sean glaring at him, raised his eyebrows in a silent challenge.

"When did you become such an asshole?" Sean asked.

Like a petulant teenager, Lee stomped off to his room, sat down in the rocker by the window and looked at the envelope in his hands. After several minutes he abruptly ripped it open. It was a handwritten letter dated two years ago.

Dearest Lee,

Today, they cut down the pine tree. I tried to reach you. I guess you didn't get my messages because I know that tree was a special thing between you and your mom, and you would've been there if you'd known about it. As they hauled it away, I realized that our rift may end up being permanent, and I may never get the chance to tell you what I need to tell you. So, I'm doing so here.

For two years after the damn doctors told your mom she'd kicked cancer, she was exhausted and in constant pain. She was one of those unfortunate people for whom chemo is particularly toxic. The harsh truth is that she was miserable most of the time. I know that when you saw her at the holidays, she put on a lively act, but that act cost her. She was in bed for weeks afterward.

So, when the cancer returned, virtually everywhere all at once, she refused to even hear about treatment options. She never saw the oncologist again. I argued with her at first, told her she had to try for me, for our family. She looked at me with such sad eyes and told me that no, she would not live her last months hidden away as the chemo finished her off. She said she'd had enough, and wanted to enjoy her time with family as best she could. Then she begged me to tell no one that the cancer had returned. She wanted to make memories without cancer overshadowing every moment.

Lee, she was my whole world. When she asked me to do that for her, I had no choice. It took everything in me not to snatch the phone from her when you said you didn't have time to come home—to tell you to get your ass home because the cancer was back. But, I couldn't because I'd promised her.

Sean saw something was wrong and confronted your mother. She made him promise, too, not to tell anyone else. That's why he got so angry with you when you said your family couldn't make it to the cabin the August before her death. I think his guilt for not telling you what was going on is why he fought so hard with you that night after her memorial.

I hope you never have to face such a situation—choosing to grant your wife's last wish or to forewarn your children about the worst loss of their lives. If I had foreseen that my promise would separate me from my eldest, God help me, son, I'm sorry but I think I would have still made the same choice. Still, I am profoundly sorry for the pain I caused you. I'm sorry, too, that my choice put a rift between you and your brothers. Even if you cannot find your way to ever forgive me, I pray that you can find your way back to your brothers.

And I'm sorry about your tree. I tried everything I could to save it.

I hope your life is filled with love, laughter, sled rides, and bonfires.

All my love,

Dad

Tears rolled down Lee's face. It was crystal clear to him: the tree wasn't just about his mom: His dad was part of all those memories. He'd missed the last five years with his dad—just like he'd missed the last few months with his mom. He'd blamed his dad, but the common denominator in all his misery was himself. The overwhelming grief and guilt of that realization choked him.

"Oh, Dad," he cried, weeping as he had not done since his mother had died. After several minutes, he felt claustrophobic; he had to get outside. He left the bedroom intending to go out on the lower deck, and found Sean still sitting in the family room. The men momentarily locked eyes, and then Lee bolted out the door.

Sean was immediately on his heels. Outside, Lee gulped the frigid air, trying to get his emotions under control. When a sob escaped him, Sean grabbed his brother's arm and pulled him into a strong embrace. Lee briefly tried to pull away, but Sean didn't let go, and eventually, Lee wrapped his arms around his brother tightly. As tiny snowflakes floated around them, Lee sobbed, "I'm so sorry…about everything."

Sean replied simply, "It's alright."

Eventually, the men broke apart, and standing in the winter air, they spoke for half an hour about their regrets and the grief they both felt over losing their parents. Finally, Sean said, "Man, I don't know about you, but I'm freezing. Let's go inside and have a drink."

Feeling shameful, Lee said, "I don't think I can face everyone."

Sean clapped his brother on the back and said, "Just walk in and say, Where's the whiskey'? It'll all sort itself out."

And it had been just that simple.

By the time the family was ready to mount their snowmobiles for their moonlit ride, the late afternoon snow flurries had cleared, and the wind had stilled. At dusk, the family began their ride to Thomas Rock Overlook.

Lee lifted the visor of his helmet to feel the frosty air on his face. The purpose of their ride was sorrowful, but Lee couldn't help but feel the exhilaration of traversing the wintery wonderland on his sled. Too soon the ride was over, and they parked their sleds and hiked the brief distance to the overlook above.

Ben suggested that as the oldest, Lee should release their dad's ashes. Lee thought about it a moment, and then said, "How about we release them together?"

So, in the deep chill of a northern Michigan winter evening with the waning moon illuminating the scene, the three brothers stepped to the edge of the overlook. Each had a hand on the urn as Lee removed its lid. As they tilted the urn, a rising breeze caught the ashes and sent them skyward, and when the last of John's ashes drifted away, a neon green glow erupted and spread in waves across the horizon. The family was awestruck, and Ben cried, "There he goes!"

Then, a fuchsia wave of light rose below the green, and Lee said in a choked voice, "And there's Mom, come to get him."

The brothers wrapped their arms around each other's shoulders and watched the Northern Lights sendoff for their dad. The colors, vibrant and shimmering in the thin winter air, were reflected in the still snow and lit the faces of the gathered mourners.

Eventually, Sean said, "How about we go back and build a bonfire?"
Lee added, "And drink Irish cocoa."

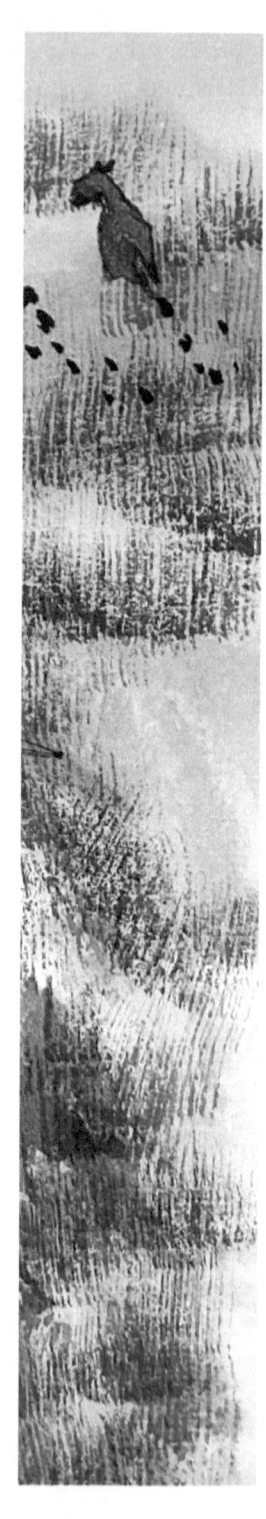

Late December

Anthony Doyle

Christmas lights run like zippers across the streets.
Open them and the elves jump out,
pimping happy mannequins in reindeer storefronts.

Away in a manger lies little Horus, in godswaddle,
The sun is born, its big ship returns.
The first rays of its sails peek above the monoliths,
taking aim. The truest aim, of course, is a willing target.

In the bar-lit lanes, a blowjob 'neath the mistletoe.
Peace be with all humankind, the Evergreen
comes in from the woods, shakes the snow
from its mighty back and stands tall in the corner.

Life lives. Death dies.

The electric fruits of fairy lights
bejewel the pine. Later in the year,
its wood will make a cross, or a sun ship.
A gallows or a burning stake.

Life dies. Death lives.

Bacchus was born on a not-so-silent night
Surrounded by braying, bleating beasts.
The days can only get brighter now.
The darkest dark is gone, the dearth recedes,
So let the wine flow, and all the other bloods.

Roman Saturnalia, Germanic Yule
Deck the halls on Modranicht,
"ubi nunc natale Domini celebramus"
said Bede, so Hark the Herald Angels sing
a Ding Dong Dandy Christmastime to you,
For there is joy for every age.

Blundra's Anatomy

Anthony Doyle

I have a black-walled womb
With gneiss folds and mud floes
It's all bark too, with trickles of sap
and latex, incubated circles,
and encircled squares, triangles rhombed
in still reflections.
Often, it loses labyrinths
down white rabbit-holes. Yes
I have a black-walled womb
that fosters growth and provides product.
Things run screaming from its gates;
Tumble from its mouth, half drowned.
I lick them clean, like foals.

I have a gaseous heart
It draws me around itself, holds me about it
in constellate organs, and ribbons of vessel,
in spools of nerve. Such is its gravity.
It throws me around it in expansions of skin,
all flare and mass, as it speaks bright,
and darkens. Speaks bright, and darkens.
Speaks bright, as I spin on my axis,
up-and-down, left-and-right.

I have a teetering brain,
a stacked favela of wind-etched whistles.
Proof that all sound is the marriage
of shape and shapelessness.
What do they see, those windows?

SOLSTICE

They see me, beheld in existence,
the condensate of eyes.
I try to remember that memory imagined
what fantasy would have me forget.

But I am a black-walled womb
Warmed by a red-ball heart,
primal swamp-life caked in brain.

And my bones are of fossilized trees.

Blundra Abides

Anthony Doyle

Lofts keep you aloft
Apartments keep you apart
Houses keep you semi, or wholly,
      detached.
Townhouses keep you in town
Madhouses, mad.
Flats keep you flat.

And in these dwellings, dwellers:
      pent-up in penthouses,
      winging around mansions
      hidebound in hideouts,
      trapped in trailers
      forgotten in ghettoes.
Dwelling, dwelling, dwelling
From Old English dwellan:
      "to lead into error, deceive,"
From the Proto-Germanic dwelana,
      "Go astray".
So we lost our way in haimlets and tuns,
We went astray staying still.

Now Blundra, if she is to abide an abode,
It has to be a yurt, a ger on a deck,
On the lakeshore.
Surrounded by evergreens.
She may have a Turkic or Mongol soul,
Or perhaps she just likes round things:
her personal circus with a mandalaic roof:

Blundra's yurt, all clad in blue,
the inside lattice painted white.

41

Her rafters, deepest red; red raw,
and stained to black in moonlight.
Coursing through those larch wood veins,
All of gravity's outward thrust
Waterproofed in stormplain skins,
Impervious to gale or gust.
No frame unturned, no post uncarved.
The yarns alive with woven lore,
Each surface thrums with myth and tale,
tabletop, bookshelves, door.
Skins and pelts on wooden floors
offer cushy furs to feet,
in wintertime, when cold winds blow,
a firewood stove provides the heat.
Outside, moon seed and oleander
stand among the saskatoon,
and Blundra rocks on wicker chairs
to while away the afternoon.
Hers would be a simple life,
Of blithe contentment with her lot.
Crapping in an outhouse
and peeing in a pot;
She'd shag her way across the floor
And sleep in a deep soft cot.
Not off the grid, but fueled by sun,
Blundra casts her spells of code
Curating shows of publate life,
Fracking the psychic motherlode.

On summer mornings, lake top mist
—where air and water meet in blur—
curls among the shoreline trunks
and tended beds of larkspur.
There's always poison,
          always threat,
Life's little nod to death,
which never skips a queue,
          but always waits its turn.
So Blundra, like some Celt or Sioux,
sets a bonfire, lets it burn.

Fish Dinner

Katharine Valentino

For someone born in Florida, raised in Georgia, Texas, and Louisiana, and residing in Southern California, a visit to Angola, Indiana, in January is a revelation. The so-called "blizzard box" is well stocked with coffee, bread, butter, powdered milk, and cans of chicken noodle soup, so there will be something to eat during the days when the snowplow can't make it all the way out to the house. The talk among neighbors shoveling hip-deep snow out of their driveways in the morning is about the idiot who left home last Monday without hat or gloves, had car trouble, tried to walk to a gas station, and was found on Thursday frozen as solid as the ice on Lake James.

Nobody had to check the ice report this morning: The ice on the lake is now so thick that if you were only a little crazy, you could drive a car on it.

The nearest neighbor, a red-cheeked shield maiden if there ever was one, shows up at my mother's door happily stamping snow off her galoshes and clapping her mittened hands in anticipation of a lovely day in fifteen-degree weather fishing out on that ice.

My mother and I spend our lovely—cozy—day inside by the fire reading James Michener.

About 5:00 that afternoon, as the sun is going down and the temperature is dropping to 9, we hear a thud outside. We open the door and discover a largish, grayish, roundish fish, still as death, on the ice-covered stone steps leading to the house.

"Oh, dear," says my mother. She closes the door.

She asks me if I've ever learned to gut a fish. After all, I've been an adult for some time. I may have learned a thing or two she didn't teach me. But I say I haven't learned the first thing about butchering Pisces. I don't suggest experimenting with this one. We go back to our fire.

The next morning, the fish has been out of the water for something like fifteen hours and presumably is continuing to solidify out there on the steps. During breakfast in her toasty kitchen, Mama says, "We should do something about that fish." Neither of us makes the first move.

By evening, Mama's feeling guilty. "We really should do something about that fish," she says. She opens the door, marches up to it, heaves it up off the ice, and extends it in my direction. "We" apparently means "I."

"Well," I say doubtfully, "maybe if I wash some of the snow off, at least we'll be able to see it better." I carry it over to the sink and turn the cold water on.

Now, before I continue, remember: This is Northern Indiana. Where the banks of snow left by the snowplow are eight feet high on both sides of the road. Where last winter, not just one but three idiots disappeared and weren't found until the springtime thaw. Where even the most careful boys do drive girls straight across the lake to dances at Pokagon State Park instead of taking forty minutes to encircle the lake to get there. To put it plainly, it's cold. Deep, dead cold.

I balance the frozen fish on two cupped hands and run it back and forth under the water. It feels not quite like an ice cube, more gelid, like one of those packets people buy to keep things cold in an ice chest. It feels heavier than 16 inches of muscle could possibly be. As the snow is rinsed off its scales, I see its glacial eye.

I move to my right to put the fish down on the counter when all of a sudden, it gives this great *thrump*. I scream. The fish launches off my hands in an explosive twist, sails halfway across the kitchen, narrowly missing Mama's head, and lands with a huge smack on the linoleum. Mama screams and recoils all the way to the refrigerator. The fish makes like one of those whirligig things in cartoons where everybody gets hypnotized. We stand there and stare at it.

After a while, I say, "I guess it's not dead."

When we can stop laughing, I use a towel to pick the creature up and cast it back outside.

The next day, the neighbor comes by again, shedding ice and snow on my mother's carpet, and asks us why the fish is still out there, and we haven't yet had a fish dinner. We explain. She snorts, calls us "weak, worthless women," takes the fish home with her and the next day brings back two perfect filets.

It's okay. She brings my mother fish; my mother does her mending.

Ice Fog

Morgan Golladay

Ice fog
coats the highway;
black ice and rime thicken
on windshield, gravel, and sidewalk.
I wait.

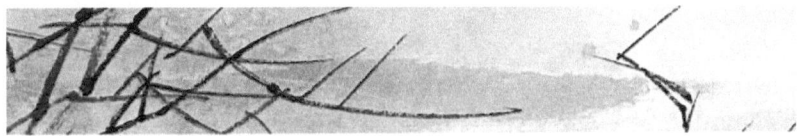

Absolution

Morgan Golladay

The absolution of the morning star
soothed my brow
as I rose from my dreams of you.
we were young,
and playful,
and in love with each other's eyes
and fingertips
and souls.
I had slept that night,
feeling the memory of your breath
stirring the hair on my neck,
the sensuousness of your presence
lulling me into a peace
I had not known for some time.
And I received forgiveness
for wishing it were
eternally and only mine.

The Day Arose Cold

Morgan Golladay

The sun rose
into a pink sky,
pausing
to gain strength
before entering this frozen day.
Yesterday's snow
is untrodden
by the small ones,
searching for food.
Even squirrels
have forsaken their branches
for warmth and safety
in their leafy nests.
Would that I, too, could stay,
snug and cozy,
but there is snow to move,
feed to put out,
animals to tend.

December Mist
Morgan Golladay

There,
at the edge of Vincent's wood,
morning fog
is lifting off pastures
covered with winter stubble.
Sunlight reflects blue
off the banded mist,
begotten by yesterday's
warm sun on December earth.
The gods of soil and field
slumber still,
cold slowly settling into their bones.

I walk the verge, waiting, watching.
My duties are elective,
my life linear,
unlike the seasons.
I greet this Solstice
with calm, measured footsteps,
waiting and watching
as cycles turn.

The Longest Shortest Day
Mary Beth Romeo

"What is the winter solstice anyway?" I ask.

"It's the most depressing day of the year," she replies as she lights a cigarette and channels my mother just to haunt me. "It's the shortest day of the year, really."

"Let's hope so," I say from the side of my mouth, the way my mother would.

I had picked Kate up from Logan airport. She had never flown to Logan, and I had not been to Boston in years. What an occasion to return. Before we get far, Kate makes me stop to check the GPS and make sure that we are going north and not south. "No repeats of last time," she says, and I shake my head.

"Your brothers are a fucking mess," I say. "They're too high to know what's going on. Did Marie tell you?" Kate nods. "They were kicked out for making a scene. I have never heard of getting kicked out for making a scene. But if anyone can do it..." Kate nods again. "It was a total abortion," I say. Kate laughs. "You trust me," I ask more seriously. "That this is right."

"Of course I do," she says, and I look sideways at her because I can hear her regret.

"You didn't miss anything," I lie.

"You're lying," she says truthfully. "But I don't have the heart to tell the boys. That it's their fault. Forever. That I was late." I say nothing. I especially don't try to smooth things over the way I usually do.

We decide to take the long way in opposition to all things cut short—daylight hours, and things more precious. Besides, nothing was going to happen until we got there. "Remember Grandma's going away party?" I ask to make my sister feel better about failed goodbyes. Kate spits out her coffee laughing. It is a warm sight on the gloomiest of

49

days, and it feels like a scene from a movie. For a moment, this story could be about other, fictitious people, and their darkest days.

"Are you excited to meet the baby?" Kate asks.

"Right," I say. "The old one-in one-out rule."

The long way means stopping at a pond somewhere in New Hampshire. I thought it was New Hampshire anyway, but I have never been able to find it again on a map. But it's a place that will do nicely as the space for future haunts. It has a lot of gray sky, browning greens, the kinds of trees that really underscore the throes of winter, and frozen tubes of goose shit everywhere. It is freezing cold and perfect for a cig. My ice coffee is too frigid to hold in my hands, and I have two kinds of jitters; only one is for the caffeine.

We get back in the car and play songs like cutting ourselves with memories. We arrive in Lebanon, New Hampshire, and run errands as a way to make long days shorter, and short days more bearable. We sit in the car for a while, like waiting for storms to pass, even though ours is imminent and not the kind that settles swiftly. We distract ourselves with a dog, one car over, whose tongue is stuck hanging from his mouth like a piece of gum that has lost its flavor. "It's actually a neurological condition," a woman walking by snaps at us. She has little patience, it seems, for the things that are grotesquely adorable to my sister and me. We nod. We grimace in unison. I speak from the side of my mouth first: "What's wrong with her?"

"Maybe her mom is dying," Kate replies, and I giggle.

We call everyone as we make our way inside, like it would be weeks and not minutes until we see them next. But we want stories like the stuff of confessionals. How was Frank? Is Marie still on one? Al and Phil—are they allowed to enter? Once we arrive—past checkpoints and elevators and double doors—all latent panics resolve themselves, as vision replaces imagination, and somehow it is both worse and not so bad in comparison. Everyone is already here because we are late. Because we are the ones trying to lengthen things for a change. Al is drunk. Phil is high on who-knows-what. Marie has her new baby, and I know immediately that I could give a shit for babies, new or otherwise. Frank has brought his wife. She will leave before long; she doesn't belong here and she knows it. *Is that everybody?* I wonder, as I look around. It feels like someone is missing, but I count six siblings from the bottom up.

"It was her birthday yesterday," Phil reminds us. That is his job—birthday reminders.

"Don't even tell her that," Marie mumbles, afraid that she can hear us. "She hated getting old."

"Well that's an interesting way to avoid it," I say, and I realize that I am channeling my mother again.

I take a peek in my mother's direction. She looks like a mummy covered in electrodes. Her eyes follow me like the eyes of a haunted portrait, and I wonder if the boys were right to get themselves ejected. Phil wants to demonstrate what happens when he holds up the signs he made for her—large love notes like oversized crosswords, and prompts to blink her eyes "yes" or "no." Frank shakes his head like the prompts were made for him, but his seniority goes without saying so Phil puts his signs away.

The rest of the day passes just as it might, except for its odd length. We order bar food and the stuff is cut in quarters like hors d'oeuvres at a wedding. "Another going away party?" Al asks between the cocktails he makes in his fifty-cent water bottle. His vodka cran has the coloring of a drop of blood in urine.

The mood shifts when we sit around the long table with everyone who's anyone around here. I would have never guessed that death wards had rooms with long tables, but here we were, sitting and shrugging and nodding the bitter truth. Frank still tries to protect the younger ones, as if they were not old enough to tell him to go fuck himself.

"Well, I for one have seen enough not to be there," I say, and everyone knows I am being an asshole. Kate and Phil, the youngest, insist on the task.

When we reconvene around my mother's bed, we are warned of minutes, hours, days—but also certainty. We spend the time with lights low, machines off, Al drunk and asleep on the floor, stirring aggressively every few minutes like he might have missed something.

"Go back to sleep," I tell him. "I promise we'll wake you."

The rest of us move about like a video montage of the various locations and positions available to one who waits. I try my hand at a Cryptoquote I found in a newspaper I lifted from the waiting room, and I think that my mother is haunting me when I complete the thing—something about picnics and Nick Nolte. I save it, slowly tearing it free, folding it small, and tucking it away. I panic when I remember that we never decided on an animal. Mostly because she only liked the ones with missing legs and eyes, or heart conditions. I feel rushed for time so I settle on a bird, and I write the word cardinal on a piece of paper. I regret my decision immediately because I wonder at my mother's fear of heights. My mind settles its worry with the thought of asking her later. I am boldening the letters of "cardinal" when some swap-out nurse enters to say that it's almost that time.

"Is it still today?" I ask. "Or is it tomorrow yet?"

"Today," the nurse replies, and I can't believe how long the shortest day can be. I take my bolded word and place it as high as I can, atop some life-saving piece of machinery that looms overhead as a joke. That will do.

We play Frank Sinatra, on a CD player of all things. "My Way," is the song, and we are all destroyed trying to imagine if the song is totally right or totally wrong for our mother. But something about us all standing here makes the final determination.

Every breath she takes is minutes apart from the next. For hours, it goes on like this. She could have been dead one hundred times over by now, but we all knew when her last bit of air comes and does; we don't need the machines or the nurses to tell us that she is gone. Because she is there. Then she is everywhere. Then Marie says, "Can you feel that," and I don't take my eyes from my mother to know that we all could.

And then she is nowhere.

The nurse comes to corroborate the information of my mother's winking out, which was almost insulting. The time of death is announced like archaic protocols, and surprisingly it is only two minutes into the second longest day of the year. Whatever day that is.

What is the winter solstice, anyway?

A Winter Welcome
Lynn Aprill

We started watching the pond because of the fish head—
fresh, frayed—which walked through our front door
in the middle of winter, clenched between our puppy's teeth.

We soon discovered grisly discarded heads
ringing an open hole in the frozen pond.
Fascinated, we started a vigil,

hoping to discover the culprit.
Our next clue–a meandering track
through recent snow. Then, one morning,

bold as sunrise, an otter sat upright on the dock,
full fish clasped in his furry front paws,
munching happily on his catch of the day.

Thus began the daily ritual of watching "our otter"
slide from his den beside the creek, cross our five-acre field,
slip into the open water, and emerge with breakfast.

Fat and sleek, he was emptying
our pond of stocked fish and filling
our mornings with anticipation.

New Year's COVID Eve

Lynn Aprill

We bundle around the bonfire—
not too close, to it
or to each other—watching

six-foot spaces expand
and contract. Our friend
apologizes more than once—

More people came, I didn't know—
as the chill air whisks virus molecules
into the flames, up to the full moon.

Rather than longing for society,
this distancing has me forgetting
how to socialize, grasping for words

like soap bubbles, floating
just beyond my fingertips. Back home
I dream of new years past, when

we would rush back to celebrate
each other before the countdown, but now
distancing finds us across the spread

of a bed gone cold from COVID
or lack of libido—
I've forgotten which.

Winter Scene

Lynn Aprill

We press   wet noses
     to bus windows, watching

saucer flakes   falling slowly from slate,   obscuring
     road,   ditch,   field.   Slowing,
     we slip into place at the end   of the driveway
     screech open
     the door,   and tumble loose   as eager pups.

     Red   petals
dot fresh snow,   leaving
     a Hansel and Gretel trail
     for us to follow.   Frosted roof
     and shrubs sheathed
     in spun sugar

and blood—
     so much blood—
     a red Nile   from front door straight
     through kitchen   and beyond.

     Our world
     a shaken snow globe,   our panic rises
     until Mom appears.

Then we learn of drifting
     lanes,   a head-on crash,   our house
     a safe shelter

as ambulances braved the bluster   and gathered up
     the wounded
     (but not dead,
     no, not dead,
     thank God).

SOLSTICE

While waiting for our universe   to settle   back into place,
        we notice
                the crumpled car,
                        mute steering wheel,
                                the perfect "O"
                                of missing glass.

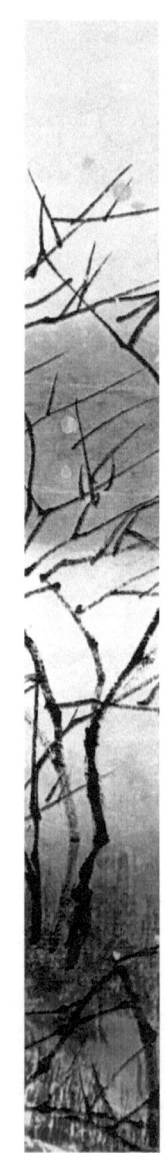

A Little Christmas

Kim DeCicco

"Merry Christmas, Mom."

It's December 21, the winter solstice, and I am filled with cheer, having just trimmed the tree. Sparkling lights inspire my greeting, chase away shortest-day gloom.

She smiles at me from her favorite armchair. Its large floral pattern a reminder of warmer days and the lush summer gardens she'd coax back to life in spring. As usual, her hands are busy creating. This time, a blue throw for my aunt, a gift that she'll complete by the holiday.

Also as usual, one of our cats, Ree-Ree, officially named Marie Antoinette, is tucked snugly between her and the chair side, one furry paw atop my mother's agile hand as if guiding each crocheted stitch—their faithful evening ritual.

Traditionally, we unpacked decorations the day after Thanksgiving to give ourselves an entire month to deck our halls and delight in the season. For weeks we'd rock around with Brenda Lee while wrapping evergreen garlands around every post and banister. Bing and Elvis would croon about white and blue Christmases as I affixed strings of miniature white bulbs to window moldings with flat golden tacks—my thumb felt bruised for days. Exterior doors and every shrub fronting our home were also illuminated to brighten chilly December nights.

Our four-foot tree, set on top of a low table, glittered with an abundance of pink and mother-of-pearl ornaments, each hung with mindful precision. Of course, those decorations were only placed after we wove *four hundred* mini lights in and out of each tree branch, the glow certain to rival any star that might shine over Bethlehem.

The week before Christmas saw our kitchen strewn with measuring cups, baking sheets, and ingredients by the pound. A fine layer of flour settled on every surface, whitening our dark wooden table and our hair. Aromas of cinnamon and chocolate whetted the appetite as a total of thirty dozen cookies baked. I squished together butter and sugar by hand—the best way, according to my mother—until they became a heavenly scented velvet grit. I gloried in the savory joy of licking each finger clean once my mother took the bowl to add eggs and flour. Every aunt, uncle, cousin, or friend who came to our home on Christmas Eve, and those who visited before or after, received a small tray of cookies wrapped in red or green cellophane. Great-Aunt Marie once left hers behind and made her husband turn the car around.

"We had to come back," she said. "Freddy won't share his, and who knows if I'll be here next December!" She was eighty-two that last year.

Our custom was to take turns opening presents on Christmas Eve. The "audience" loaded plates with sausage and peppers, stuffed shells, and crackers topped with port wine cheese from the buffet in our kitchen. The youngest generation also snuck pieces of ribbon candy from overflowing bowls, while adults balanced plates with one hand and sipped manhattans with the other. Ree-Ree and her brother, Casanova, seized crumpled balls of wrapping paper then climbed under the tree, thrilled with their plunder and the safety of camouflage.

But now Christmas is a smaller affair. There are fewer decorations, and I wait until the solstice to adorn my house.

"Merry Christmas," I say again, and touch my mother's face. Fingertips meet the cold glass of a picture frame. Memories shrivel as a chill runs from my hand up my arm. I place the frame holding my mother and Ree-Ree next to others surrounding my two-foot tree, with its twenty lights and seven tiny ornaments. In one photograph I see my father and brother posing on a dock overlooking New York's Lake George. In a second, my grandmother and great aunt and uncle stand together in our yard during a July 4 party. A third shows another aunt and uncle cutting cake on their wedding day. In the last and smallest photograph, Casanova sniffs a red rose.

I look at my cousin, Richie, who settles beside me on the sofa. He offers a cracker smeared with port wine cheese and a freshly poured manhattan.

"Wanna open presents early and get drunk?"

I laugh, shrug, clink my glass to his. "Why not?" What difference does it make if we celebrate tonight or in three days? I turn up the carols then go in the kitchen to preheat the oven. "Let's have stuffed shells too."

Hibernation

Buffy Aakaash

These outdoor smells
of nature chilled
beckon the bear in me,
a winter call
to hunker down
and dream.

And in this seasonal drag
I wonder
in my doing,
  pulling in,
what I will not be doing,
In my thinking,
  letting out,
what I will not be thinking.

I think,
inhaling thoughts,
and release circles of smoke
into the belly of the beast.

I grieve,
  pulling in,
what will be left undone,
  and let out
these ruminations feeding
my hunger in sleep,
  pulling in emptiness,
  grateful for the quiet.

On Lake Washington: The Duck

Buffy Aakaash

The silence
upon which these feathers
float is the wishing well
for my pending altruism,
the wish itself the stillness
which drifts from its center
like fog from the heavens
inter-coursing the city
with its mysterious
elongated mood.
I feel in her there
this body
flowing with hers.
When she dives
she eats the quietude
of cold winter waters,
at the surface spits it out,
a fish in her mouth
for those of us
come to the edge,
to goad us from the nest.

Beneath the Stars I Release

Buffy Aakaash

The moon rising later
gives me more time
with the stars.
Brittle cold glass
shattering air cuts
my time beneath them.

I ponder my release as it
                bubbles then puddles.

Will it freeze solid overnight?
Melt and mortify into unpleasant
aromas in the spring?

In a tooth-cracking breeze
I shake, close myself up,
and go back to the fire inside.
Take comfort there.
Think of warm friends.
Hot times.

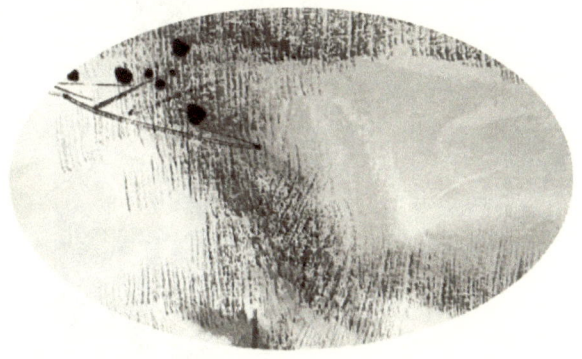

The Christmas Stockings
Mary Salome

Catherine didn't ask for much. When her mother invited her to Christmas and asked if there was anything she wanted, she felt silly saying yes. She had just turned forty-eight, and though the divorce had left her feeling a particular kind of vulnerability, she didn't want to bring that home for the holidays. The whole point of the divorce was to try to finally grow up.

"I can't think of anything," she said, switching the phone to her left hand so she could lock the door behind her with her right. Her mother had a habit of calling just as she was leaving for work. "I don't need any more stuff, Mom."

"Well, you have to get something."

"How about some socks?" Catherine said.

"Socks?"

"Yeah. With polar bears on them. Or penguins in scarves. Something cheerful."

"Well, okay. We're just excited you're coming. Teresa just said she can get time off as well."

Catherine paused. The corners of her mouth turned down and she shrugged, glad her mother couldn't see her. Her whole face felt the pull of gravity toward the black hole in her chest. For about a year, her life had slowly collapsed into the dense cavity that occupied her ribcage. It swallowed desire first, then creativity, and would have swallowed her job if she hadn't been able to do her work in her sleep. Even her complex feelings toward her sister Teresa had been pulled in, like tiny iron filings toward a magnet.

"Great," she said.

Three months later, sitting between her mother and sister on the couch in front of the Christmas tree, she couldn't remember how that phone conversation had ended. The black hole in her chest had traveled with her for the holidays, but no one else seemed to notice. Teresa had flown from Europe for the first time in three years with a vortex of her own. It sucked not light, but attention. She wore cashmere and silk. She had neighbors on the ramblas who made too much noise. She made over two hundred thousand Euros a year and claimed it was hardly worth the exhaustion of managing a team of over two hundred on multiple continents. Just days ago, when Catherine put down a bottle of perfume in a shop downtown after looking at the price, Teresa marched to the counter and bought it for her.

Catherine handed out the gifts she'd brought and quietly unwrapped the packet her mother handed her. Two pairs of plain grey socks, devoid of polar bears and penguins. The black hole inside of her belched out a sour trickle of something old but nameless. She hardly asked for anything, and when she did, no one heard.

"Thanks, Mom," she said, holding them up for everyone to see. From some distant place she recognized they were actually quite nice—soft wool, crew length. She conjured a sweet feeling and tried to force it to her face.

"I can't believe it!" Teresa said, unwrapping a similar packet and pulling out a pair of socks. They were knee-length and black. "These are boot socks!"

"Yes," their mother said, sipping her coffee.

"I asked for crew-length socks! I can't wear these." In her outrage she pulled her plush fleece bathrobe tighter around her collar. "You got Catherine crew-length socks."

"Oh," their mother said. She listed a little in her chair. "Catherine, give Teresa your socks."

"What?" Catherine asked.

Her mother reached for them and exchanged them for Teresa's.

"She makes thousands of Euros per year, but she has to have my socks." Catherine felt her chest rattle with tiny iron shavings shaking loose from their moorings. They shook their way up her throat and filled her mouth, cutting the tender inside of her cheeks.

"They're just socks," her mother said, reinflating and starting to look angry.

"Every time she has a feeling, we have to placate her," Catherine said.

"You've got to be kidding," her mother said.

Catherine stood up and threw the black socks at her sister. "I'm going for a walk," she said, pulling her boots onto her feet and a coat over her pajamas. She came back an hour later and dressed quickly for the holiday party her aunt and uncle were hosting in Boston. Their mother didn't say much as she drove. Catherine sat in the back seat cradling the Christmas cookies her mother had baked, while Teresa sat in front and quietly noted that the coffee was much better in Spain.

Soups (A Lost Book of the Bible)

Robert Fleming

1 There came a time when the people of Campbell found their vat empty. The people cried out to the Lord, *Lord why have you let our vat go dry?* The water in the vats separated from the broth. The people spooned their prayers. But the Lord did not bring forth soup.

2 The people abandoned idols and turned to the Lord. All of the idols of Rain had been destroyed. The Lord repurposed Rain from a water maker to a soup maker. Rain, as she released water, onto the earth, was called by the Lord. Rain, you've been a releaser of water, come with me and be a maker of soup. Rain followed the Lord and became the soup maker of Campbells.

3 Later, in the time of Christ, Mary Magdalen washed Christ's feet. Mary to make ends meet worked as the whore of Nazareth and made soup. Mary was boiling water and herbs and soup splattered onto Mary's eyes. When Mary washed Jesus feet, Mary cried. Mary's tears souped onto Jesus' feet. When men strained Mary, Jesus souped, whose veins are filled with blood, and not soup, shall not spoon the last of the soup.

4 Jesus was in Galilee and entered a walking on water contest. While Jesus won the competition, he was dethroned. It was proven, that Jesus did not walk on water, Jesus walked on soup. Jesus, before the walking, spooned mushroom soup, onto the sea of Galilee. The mushrooms separated, from the soup, and formed mushroom pads. Jesus walked on mushrooms pads. It was the soup and not the water. Herod reclaimed Jesus crown of soup.

5 Still the people's vat was empty. Despite that Mary and Jesus had performed the miracles of the soup. The people asked Jesus to give the sacrament of the soup. But Jesus souped not. Jesus said, I am the only soup of Christ. The people disobeyed the Lord and went to the shores of Galilee. With a ladle, the people hit the rock of soup. Soup came forth. When the ladle hit the rock it made the first percussion. God was angry because he/her was the only one allowed to create. The Lord punished her/his children. For forty years the Lord made his/her children follow the Soup of Campbell, until they reached a new bowl, the soup of Progresso.

not stopping by roadkill on route 66

Robert Fleming

route 66 I've driven a thousand times
the sports bar at exit 289
you will not see me brake here
to claim this creature- is alive? I fear

my car's heater is not heating
to stop at the roadside for a pee
without a car repair shop near
I will pass these meals to my rear

a roadkill must be eaten in 48 hours
any more stomach sickness follows
roadkill death time detector in my trunk
butchering I flunked

my headlights snow show a deer
get sugar giving this deer to my dear
red and blue lights circling in my rear
miles to be chased before I gulp more beer

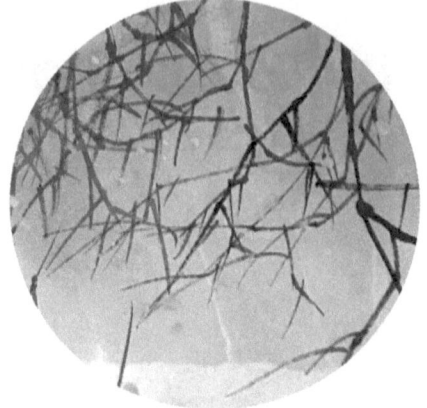

Benvenuti, tutti!

Alan Bern

~in memory of Anna Tasca Lanza, died July 12, 2010

Benvenuti, tutti! Welcome everyone! Fifteen years ago my wife and I returned from a sublime winter vacation in Sicilia. Sicilia, homeland to so many different peoples for 10,000 years and to many Americans right now, a homeland not exactly mine, but a homeland in my heart. I must tell you that I am considering changing my name…to…Misterbianco. Please say it with me, Mister Bianco. Funny name, Misterbianco, Mister White: it's actually a town on the lower slopes of the volcano, Etna, the largest live volcano in Europe, covered with winter snow as we saw flying in from the west, but then, no snow visible, with the cloud-cover on the east as we drove from the Catania

airport on the Tangenziale to the Circonvallazione CT, the rim road circling around the grand City of Catania, mad traffic all around us.

Misterbianco, it could mean white mystery. So I thought. Appropriate, too, when there is snow on the mountain, a headless monster covered with a white vest, il saio bianco. In English, though, I try hard not to think of R. Crumb's Whiteman, Mister Bianco, uptight asshole who finally loosened up by escaping civilization and engaging in some positions <u>not</u> for public consumption, not a bad idea that, but impossible I am sure; that is, impossible to escape civilization.

Heh, heh. Misterbianco, population 44,695, a town on its own with several lovely baroque buildings, but also a *sobborgo di Catania*, a Catanian suburb. Ah, living under a huge live volcano and driving in impossible traffic into and out of Catania to work each and every day. Sublime!

In fact, however, the name Misterbianco derives from the Sicilian term *Musteri jancu*, that means *monastero bianco* (white monastery), and it refers to the white walls of a pre-existent Benedictine monastery, destroyed in the large 1669 eruption, by Mount Etna's lava flow.

Okay then. But before I rush off to the Franz Kafka Meta-Memorial Name-Change Bureau, to don my new name, Misterbianco, I want to tell you one story from the middle of our trip.

After adventures in Catania and on the East Coast of Sicilia, we drove our rented car toward the center of Sicilia, to its heartland. We were to take cooking lessons from the great chef and writer, the Marchesa Anna Tasca Lanza of Regaleali, a Country Estate, yes, but also a fine, fine winery, run by her brother, handed down from his father. Regaleali does not sound exactly Italian so it must be a Sicilian word meaning 'regal.' Right? Way wrong. It is from the Arab *rahal Ali* meaning village (or home) of Ali. Whoa, there, Sicilia, what of your heritage over these 10,000 years. The Arabs came in the midst of the 1st millennium CE and left so much. One thing they absolutely left was the sweet-and-the-sour in the amazing Sicilian cuisine. So the Marchesa emphasized in her lessons. But wait, I have forgotten to tell you that as we drove over the autostrada and then onto a smaller road and then a narrower lane of potholes and curves, it began to snow. We began to climb, and it began to snow some more. Okay, this is Winter, but this is also Sicilia, and we were not in what Sicilia calls its mountains. But it snowed. And it snowed. And we called the Marchesa on our cellphone: she said the roads were fine, and we'd get through. We drove, and it snowed, and they started to get slippery, and we called again. We talked to her husband, Vincens. We were getting close now, but we were at a fork that he couldn't quite recognize from our description. Finally, somehow, though their directions were not quite there, we arrived at the Estate, at Regaleali. It snowed through our lovely dinner that she prepared, and I watched her prepare. And it snowed the next day. She had never seen snow like this at Regaleali in her 72 years, nor heard of it snowing like this, and her family had been there for 175 years. That night we ate a lovely baked chicken covered with herbs collected from the Estate and dried and basted, alternating with orange juice and white wine, the sweet and the sour; and for dessert we had *Biancomangiare* (white eat), a dish that some think the French brought to Sicilia as *Blancmange*, a pudding, in Britain, that makes a schoolboy gag. In fact, *Biancomangiare* is delicious and simple, sugar, almond milk, and cornstarch with additions of, perhaps, candied squash, coffee, pistachios, vanilla cookies, and certainly cinnamon. In fact, these puddings were and are very popular throughout the Middle East, and it is most likely that *Biancomangiare* came to Sicilia with the Arabs. It is an overwhelming white pudding with little colors of sweet and tangy flavors sitting in and poking out.

In the snowy, now icy, night, it was perfection. By now, too, we were snowed in. The Marchesa and her husband were more amazed than we. She had lived there for 70+ years, and it had never snowed like this! I had not slept so well, so deeply, in years. Safe in the warm beds, filled inside with *Biancomangiare*, snowed in.

Late last night snowed in,
we could go nowhere
but into our dreams
in the darkest rooms.
Sometime near the dawn,
one of us awoke
the other with love,
perhaps our bodies
or even a thought
sent between our two minds
like an icicle
after cracking, still.

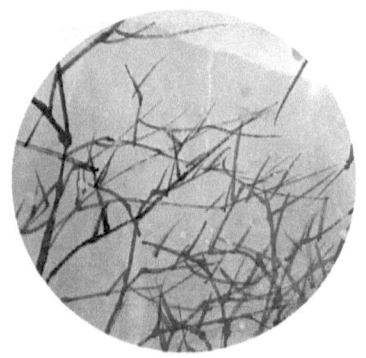

Jack Frost
Bri Gonzalez

The man is a mountain range.
I waste no time slipping into his
crags. A corpse is not a property.

He strokes me pretty like a devil,
strangles my sternum, stuffs each
organ with hail. Winter is not unlike
a staircase which is not unlike a murder.

A clenched jaw spits out snowcaps.
He craves the season, licks it off my
tongue, nips my lower lip for rime.
I beg and he worships.

Sometimes dying comes with
a reprise. Sleet-bound whimper.

If You Were Still Here for Winter

Bri Gonzalez

~for Carson Thomas Miller

you might bless my dad's flugel horn with spit, caroling door to door in that hot-mess holiday sweater I hate. You might complain about the hover and harassing of your parents, no idea how cold the missing is. No idea what a snowstorm feels like. You might make hot chocolate for whoever you're dating, cheeks burnt, milk searing through a marshmallow safety net. There would be no brick skeleton of your home, no strangers redecorating your final breath. Instead, we would commiserate lukewarm brie at a neighborhood party, and I would say we're doomed, say we peaked twelve years ago trick-or-treating as pirates. Instead, you would turn twenty-five and we would gain cranberry cheeks from a night of hearth-slurping.

We, stumbling home in the extra frozen dark, would trade smiles, imagine impossible versions of our next-December selves.

Bitter

Bri Gonzalez

I build tiny winters:
fog-smitten
hole-smeared gloves

night-kissed sweat
shivers

starting and ending
days in
patched darkness

frayed sweater
seams the thought

of your pulse under
dull streetlamps

mug-cramped
sink after

breakfast pills after
dinner pills after
mourning-

frozen photos
saved voicemails

reaching for a thought
I am unable to find

My Favorite Company Christmas Party

John Johnson

Not at the Ritz Carlton with bacon wrapped scallops and gin
martinis,
Not dressed in my Sunday best with a freshly purchased Santa Claus
tie,
Not at the Watergate with tours of Nixon's bungling burglars spy
room,
Not with a deejay who predictably played Gangnam Style every year,
No River Cruise navigating icy waters like the Titanic,
No buffet with carved roast beef with horseradish and mushroom
gravy,
No red and green macarons or cream dolloped pecan pie finger tarts,
No after-party corralling of intoxicated co-workers,
No hotel, but a fire pit in a backyard, bundled in sweatshirts and hats.
Three chairs sit in a socially distant equilateral triangle,
Minimizing the pandemic risk that thrust us into loneliness.
Laughter replacing music, Christmas cookies replacing macarons,
M&Ms are our hors d'oeuvres, hot black coffee warms us better than
bourbon,
The gift of friendship heightened by stepping out from behind a
ZOOM screen.

Dead Week

John Johnson

"The week between Christmas and New Year's Eve is a time when nothing counts, and when nothing is quite real."
  –Helena Fitzgerald

Crumpled wrapping paper
        and recycled ribbons surround
        the tree like crime tape,

Darkness oozes
        like spilled black ink
        over the fading sun,

Eating yet another
        four-day-old slice of pecan pie
        fails to satisfy,

Familial bonds
        fray from familiarity
        and flu viruses,

Gift returns tinged with guilt—
        but I haven't worn a medium
        in over twenty years,

Holiday radio stations
        convert to Cowboy Country
        faster than a bucking bull-rider,

Imbibing Old Fashioneds
        in the early afternoon
        to get drunk faster than the sun sets,

SOLSTICE

Jealousy stirred by
> Instagram photos of former friends
> on the beach in Bora Bora,

Kindness disappears
> faster than Santa's sleigh,
> as road-raging drivers cut you off,

Lists of resolutions cat-scratched
> on the back of Christmas Cards
> I will misplace before midnight,

Movie theaters filled
> with masked patrons
> and asymptomatic COVID-spreaders,

Nutcrackers look at their watches
> counting down the days till they reenter
> the witness relocation program,

Oscillating not-so-wintery temperatures
> confuse our bodies more
> than a misdiagnosing physician,

Postal workers
> attend yoga classes
> to fix their hunchbacks,

Quiet nights
> echo the abandonment
> of the city center,

Requests for charitable donations
> overflow my inbox
> like an unwatched boiling pot,

Stockings no longer hang
> by the chimney,
> with care or otherwise,

SOLSTICE

Television binge-watching
       every holiday baking program
       until they become stale,

Unique College Football Bowl Games
       hocking mortgages and potatoes
       more effectively than an infomercial,

Vacation days
       must be used before they expire at year's end
         like leftover Christmas tuna fish casserole,

Wannabee romantics
       try to steal kisses like a burglar
       on New Year's Eve,

Excess pounds
       soon to be exploited by
       excessive diet scams,

Year-end retrospectives on those we lost
       as predictable
       as death itself,

Zodiacs promise Capricorns
       a stellar alignment
       of fortunes and romance,

An abundance of angst
       Squeezed so tightly
       into just one week—

between Christmas and New Year's Day.

The Eagles Mere Toboggan Run

Virginia Watts

A few days after Christmas, my family travelled north to celebrate New Year's Eve with relatives. It was a long drive. As our car climbed up and down mountains, my ears popped and pained, and my two older brothers morphed into nonstop whine machines. Curt was always starving to death, and Mark's eardrums were about to burst and launch him into a lifetime of deafness.

After a few hours of their voice boxes, my mother's repeated chime of *stop your belly aching*, and my father's medley of Nat King Cole's top hits, I almost wished Mark's prediction would come true for all of us. I tried my best to tune everyone out until my father flicked up the turn signal lever and announced with his characteristic cheerfulness: "Pit stop, ladies and gentlemen. The borough of Eagles Mere at last!"

When we stepped out of the car, my suffering vanished. We had arrived at the top of the world. With a sky that big, it was easy to forget there was land below it. Eagles Mere had a toboggan run that started at the top of a steep hill and ended in the middle of a frozen lake. We waited for it all year, hoping the weather conditions were cold enough to freeze enough layers of lake water. Then chunks of ice could be extracted with chain saws to construct the run.

By the time we arrived, the run was about to close for the day. It would be very dark very soon. The surrounding woods were dense. We had to hurry before the night swallowed the sun if we wanted a turn. We'd grab our bulky snowsuits from the trunk. Zipper up. Fasten boots. Pull on hats, knot scarves, and trudge as quickly as Michelin Man siblings could to the top of a steep hill where adults were launching toboggans of children down the ramp.

Even though we had survived the toboggan run at twilight many times, the three of us fell silent waiting in the line. Other children were flying down the hill lightning fast, scarves flying, screaming. They sounded terrified. Our breath hung in little, anxious clouds as we watched them travel far out over the top of a cold, black mirror.

In the summer, my brothers and I swam and floated in the lake's choppy waters, rode around the perimeter in the puttering motorboat aptly named "The Barely Able." Now, underneath a thick, top layer of ice, the natural springs that renewed the lake were not at rest. The lake never froze completely even if it looked like it did. At deep depths the water flowed as freely as it did in the warm months. Native fish drummed their fins, nibbled, and tried not to bump into each other. Life was unchanged even though the lake's outward appearance was so unlike her summer self. She looked bigger for one thing, as inhospitable as the dark side of the moon. Barren trees outlined her shape as the moon's reflection shimmered on top like a giant, lonely, silver teardrop.

Just before our turn, I would glance back at the silhouette of my tall, broad-shouldered father in the leaving light. When he waved, I lifted my chin a degree higher, turned back toward the granite body of the lake, the grey wolf night above it, galloping toward me, toward everything, ravenous, ready to open his massive jaws.

It was much scarier going down at dusk, praying your toboggan wouldn't crash into another toboggan or something else you couldn't see that might be waiting out there in the middle of the lake for a fresh load of kids. And there was that additional haunt of an idea that even though all you had to do was turn around and walk back up the way you had come down, what if suddenly you didn't know where you were or recognize anything.

As my brothers scrambled eagerly aboard, I hesitated. The gyrating, orange bonfires near the docks around the lake hinted at wickedness and trickery, reminded me of the fairytale stories I had read. *The Little Match Girl. Little Red Riding Hood.* The lake itself could be a roasting pot in disguise like the pot in *Hansel and Gretel* where the bloodthirsty witch boiled children over a hearth fire and ate them for dinner. Still, I did it. I stepped forward. I lifted my arm, reached my mitten toward a bigger mitten that helped me step inside one of the high-sided, wooden toboggans.

READY! SET! GO!

Once we were off, the night swallowed the sun. After that final, mighty thrust, as soon as our toboggan was set free, the world flipped sunless, snuffed silent. My heart thumped in a vacuum as we soared downward through inky air, my body lifted off the seat, frigid air whipping my face. I heard the three of us screaming and laughing. Far away, echoey sounds. At the bottom of the hill, we clapped as our toboggan began sliding level, moving quickly over the slick surface, the smoke of the bonfire flames from the lake bank acrid in my nose, my wet exhales freezing tight on my cheeks.

When we slowed down and came to a halt, silence was all that awaited us in the middle of that lake. In heavy snowfalls, flakes landing on the snowpack around the toboggan made noise like talcum powder shaken onto the surface of a shiny porcelain sink. I'd tilt my head back, look up at stars torn lose from their anchors, swirling around each other in congratulatory, gleaming ribbons, heralding how far we had come, how far we would go.

Winter Sestina

R. David Fulcher

The fields are full of dead flowers,
Their heads bowed and heavy like shackled ghosts
Shambling towards the roadside.
Cars choke out the white noise of the sun,
Their grilles belching dirty thunder
Which burns the hand of silence.

Children sleep in flannel silence,
Their eyelids closed flowers
Which flicker beneath sensory thunder.
Snowflakes fall unnoticed, crystalline ghosts
Which haunt the reaches of the sun
Then die by the roadside.

A thousand eyes watch the roadside.
Yawns ripple the silence
As the metal tide flows towards the sun.
The cold forges the bitterness of flowers
Never bought or lovers who embrace as living ghosts.
The low, choppy skies herald no thunder.

Children scramble up slopes, their feet muffled thunder
As they speed on waxed runners towards the roadside.
The sick ones stay in, their ecstasy only a ghost
As they watch the cold celebration in windowed silence.
Lovers sleep like joined flowers,
Temporarily oblivious to the death of the sun.

SOLSTICE

Alley cats curl in newspapers, their eyes miniature suns
Which flare in time to the urban thunder.
Children make snow-angels, the flowers
Of their cheeks red like the cans which litter the roadside.
Bums sleep on grates in silence,
Haunted by bottles, invisible as ghosts.

Cars sleep in drifts like dinosaur ghosts
waiting to be freed by salt and sun.
A film of ice covers all as the silence
Lowers and blankets cover the thunder
of hearts. Empty, the roadside
Sighs and dreams of flowers.

The ghost of the sun waits behind the thunder,
Shedding petals of fire
Which collect silently by the roadside.

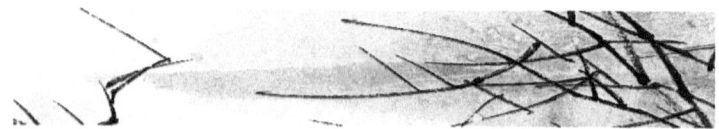

The Dead of Winter
William F. Crandell

"I swear I had no idea it would be a whorehouse when I stepped into that place yesterday to get warm and to buy a *Bible* in Spanish, or that two people would get their brains blown out. Thirty degrees and snowing like a son of a—well, snowing hard as hell." The old guy looked more embarrassed than scared. "My wife slapped me and tossed me out of the house. Two days after Christmas! I need a private eye, Mr. Griffin."

Professor Joseph Scalzo had slunked into my office that morning—Tuesday, December 28, 1948, if anybody cares—like a whipped lapdog, closing behind his short, tubby body the door that said "Aadlund & Griffin Investigations" on the frosted glass. We sat down, the old man on the once-bright blue couch facing my Army surplus desk. His sodden raincoat drizzled from the wooden chair to the floor. Beyond the frosted windowpanes, a sky of steel wool showered down rain again. Yesterday had been worse: an inch of snow paralyzed the nation's capital. Now the temperature waltzed around freezing, and a sharp wind kept sleeting razor blades. Today, Washington being a town where even the weather has opinions, the late morning ranged four or five degrees higher.

"Slow down, Doctor Scalzo." I kept my voice low, my right hand up like a traffic cop. A fresh case would help me out of the financial doldrums between Christmas and New Year's. "Let's start at the beginning, okay?"

Dr. Scalzo had a can opener nose and the body of a teapot, short and stout. He looked about sixty-five. "I'm the sole suspect," he explained, "in a fatal double shooting yesterday. I recently retired as a professor of Spanish Literature at Catholic University, so I take a long walk daily to keep my weight down."

Doesn't seem to be working, I thought.

"After lunch," he went on, "I hiked to Mount Vernon Square, then trudged off toward those pathetic little shops on Ninth Street, the ones with trusses and old women's shoes. There's a tobacco store around Constitution Avenue that sells my favorite stinky cigars."

"And—"

A crash of lightning startled us, an artillery barrage just above our heads, followed by a downpour. Washington in winter.

"Well, Mr. Griffin, halfway down Ninth, the rain began pouring like now, like a son of a bitch. Just below freezing. In two, three blocks my teeth started chattering. Between two buildings with their windows papered up, I spotted a shop with its lights on. Headed for the door. In the window they had one of those mannequin hands, the kind women's shoe stores display nylon stockings on."

I nodded my head.

"Only this one," the professor adds, "has an illustrated Bible in Spanish spread open on its fingers. Well, I teach Spanish, and I needed a Spanish Bible, I'd worn out my old copy. That gave me two reasons to step inside, so in I went. Didn't notice at first how rank the place smelled, but it felt warm. Behind the counter, I saw a tall man with his back to me, kissing a young short-haired blonde woman. He ignored me, which seemed rude, but who could blame him?" He had a sneaky chortle.

"Not me," I answered.

Scalzo nodded. "I asked the fella, 'How much for that beautiful item you're advertising in the window?' and pointed back over my shoulder with my thumb. The blonde woman broke for air and told me ten bucks. 'Not bad,' I said. 'At that price, I'd like two of them.' I could keep the other at my office."

I kept trying to imagine how paying twenty bucks for a pair of expensive-looking Spanish Bibles had led to two murders. "Go on."

Professor Scalzo's upper lip got sweaty. "Suddenly I realized another woman, a red-head in a lime green sweater, stood to my right, between me and the window. 'Give Sally here the twenty,' she said in a sharp-edged voice. I paid the blonde, stuffed the window copy in my coat pocket, and followed the red-head into the back. She smiled and added, "I'll get everything ready. I'm Janie. I'll grab another one. You can wait for me in this room.' As Janie headed out of the room, she gave me a wink."

Something started feeling very odd about Dr. Scalzo's story. It must have showed in my face. "I know," he told me, shaking his jowly head.

His throat sounded dry. "Didn't feel right to me either. She touched my sleeve. 'Take your clothes off, sweetie. I'll be right back.' Damned if she didn't whisk the green sweater away, with not a lick under it."

Griffin, I told myself, your mouth is hanging open.

"Whatever Janie meant," he went on, "there'd clearly been a misunderstanding. Then I heard what could have been two shots from a small pistol and pivoted immediately toward the lobby. Stood stock-still for a minute. Nothing more happened. I didn't see anybody out in front, but a pocket-size automatic lay in front of the counter. Well, you don't leave a gun lying around, so I snatched it up. Freshly fired. I fought in the Great War, Griffin. The smell of cordite always lingers. A woman behind me screamed."

"Screamed?"

Scalzo nodded. "Then a police officer with a revolver in his right hand thrust the door wide and yelled 'Freeze!' I froze, all right, a Roman statue in the icy wind. That's when I spotted two pairs of shoes, a woman's and a man's, poking out from behind the counter. The officer snapped handcuffs on me, and a paddy wagon took me to the jail. They let me call my lawyer maybe two hours later. Took a cab home and spent the rest of the evening enduring one of Peg's shrill, mean-spirited tirades. I'd rather face cannon fire."

———

I'd never met Dr. McGarricle, the medical examiner who autopsied the two bodies. Short, friendly, in his early forties, he twiddled a dead cigar the size of a Lincoln Log and pointed to a chair that had worn out while Grant was president. "Still sleeting outside? How can I help you, Mister—um—"

"Just raining and damned cold." I handed him my card. "Griffin, Jack Griffin. I understand you did the autopsies on the brothel shooting yesterday," I said. "Can I see the report?"

McGarricle handed me a brown paper folder. "Not much there. Around 1:15 a guy walked into a storefront whorehouse off Mission Row, shot a man in the back of his skull and a woman in her forehead. Apparently the two had been kissing at the time. She'd smeared her lipstick over a swath of his face. Both of them died instantly."

I finished scanning the report. "How far was the muzzle from either of the victims?"

He sucked on his stogie. "Well, the first shot—the name was Erno

Jablonka, the chauffer for Beauregard Bragg Madison, Deputy Undersecretary of the Treasury. As I say, for the first shot, the gun wasn't quite touching, maybe two inches from the head. The woman, a prostitute named Sally Pilcher, took a round from about two feet away. No burns, Griffin."

"All right, we've got a couple kissing, somebody comes up behind the man and shoots him point blank, he drops where he stands, the woman catches bullet number two, is that right?" Autopsies often tell a simple story.

"That's right."

"Same weapon for both?" Might as well note the details.

"Oh, absolutely. Excellent matches between the gun and the slugs. So, yes, the same weapon for both killing, a run-of-the-mill Colt .22 pocket automatic with a lot of miles on it. You may think that's a small gun for an execution, but a number of professional killers use .22s. Fits in a shirt pocket, accurate and lethal up close."

I nodded, not convinced that my client fit that bill. "What else about the shooter?"

"He's short, and maybe fat. The corpulence could explain the stand-off between the muzzle and the impact. Certainly he's short. The trajectory of the first shot was thirty degrees or more upward. The victim was tall. The second shot stayed closer to the horizontal plane, but she stood shorter than her boyfriend and farther from the killer. By the way, the suspect left nice, clear fingerprints on the handle and the barrel. Matches one Joseph M. Scalzo, the principal suspect in this investigation."

Short, and maybe fat. Great. Shuffling again through the file folder, I felt my eyebrows knit. "I don't see results of a paraffin test." Gunpowder residues always clung to a shooter's gun hand.

"Yeah, I didn't either. I asked Homicide and nobody knew anything about it. They get overwhelmed during the holidays and with cops out sick."

Test's only good for a day, I thought. *Today's a day too late date.*

I jotted down the name of the arresting officer, Jimmy Cochrane, a rookie. A uniformed sergeant said "the kid" would be out on his beat until maybe suppertime.

Outside, the wind had picked sharply, the temperature had clearly dropped, and the battleship-gray sky had started sleeting razor blades. again Walking through empty, icy streets in a late December storm called for care. In two blocks, I must've seen a dozen drivers spinning their wheels on thin ice. I grabbed some watery, tepid chili, then headed toward the brothel.

Mission Row began a few blocks from where I'd parked. Bare trees bent beneath crystalline ice lining H Street. Miserable-looking pedestrians inadvertently dancing down the sidewalks, looking less funny than in movies. Most people had the sense to stay home. The drive, through blocked byways and fender-benders, took me half an hour. I oozed into a short parking spot, thankful I'd learned to drive in northern Ohio.

Noting the lack of numbers on most of the doors, I passed a sullen bar named The Hump, its juke-box more spirited than the crowd inside. An unlabeled shambles smelling of reefer smoke came next, followed by a couple of flop-houses and a ragged old man with scraped-up hands and a busted nose, snoring in a shooting gallery doorway. The door itself lay wide open.

After a boarded-up shop with smashed windows, I saw two massive firemen haul a stretcher out of the next place, a blanket pulled over the face. They slid the body into the back of an ambulance. One of the pallbearers turned to me. "Every time we get snow, idiots crack their skulls on icy sidewalks or light charcoal fires to keep warm and die from carbon monoxide, like this guy. His wife and kids are waiting for another litter. The dead of winter."

My ears felt like I could snap them off. The narrow two-story building I'd reached as looked not much wider than outhouses I'd seen on an uncle's Indiana farm. The masonry wore a good five decades of grime. The door had taken part in as many stories as Mark Twain ever wrote. In a cracked window no more than three feet square, I spotted the totemic hand, reaching.

The Spanish Bible had been replaced by a worn pair of red lace panties over the offering plastic hand. The assemblage stood on an oval-shaped rubber mat, a visual metaphor for a damsel drowning in quicksand. A gauzy curtain screened the display from whatever waited inside, and a heavier pair of opaque drapes behind the veil that had started out dark blue framed the right and left of the window. No Christmas decorations.

I pulled open the door and stepped inside, tugging my gloves off. An open bottle of Air-Wick on the counter had already lost a rearguard fight against the sour smells. Two of the hookers sat on a crimson-cushioned bench in the lobby, not terribly attractive, not uninteresting, either. Another staffed a barstool behind the counter, and the fifth rested her duff on the inside ledge of the window. That one, her Irish setter hair a mahogany red that nature rarely endows on humans, had a generous figure and I guessed her to be Janie, the one who led Professor Scalzo into the back rooms.

Not all the gloom came from weak lights and cigarette smoke. The remaining pair, bottle blondes of differing ages, tried out insincere pouts to whet my appetite. On the right, a weather-beaten temptress of fifty or so seemed she'd be equally comfortable humping a guy on dirty sheets or blackjacking him in the alley out back. The other, maybe in her late twenties, had the most saleable figure in the run-down brothel, though more modest than the other four. Still, she had a jagged face that suggested whatever she lusted for wasn't sex.

The thick-waisted old-timer on the battered barstool smiled a yellow grin. She shook a Philip Morris from its pack and stuck it between thin, pink-painted lips. "Whadye fancy, handsome? Somethin' hot to warm your cockles?"

How the hell old is this one? I asked myself. Seventy? Maybe some embers left, but still…It wasn't that none of them passed what a former sailor I knew called the desert island test, but I never bought sex. I'd have been mortally embarrassed, and these women weren't likely to excite anybody to rioting. I showed the lady at the counter a photostat of my license and said, "Right now, I'm looking for information on the shooting here yesterday. I'm told Janie Callahan came as close as anybody to seeing it."

The redhead behind me on the windowsill and stood up. "I'm Janie Callahan, honey. How can I—uh—satisfy you?" She wore a clingy green sweater that might have been the one the professor described her whipping off, and a button-front wool skirt unfastened halfway to her crotch.

I pulled my eyes level with hers. "I'm investigating the shooting of Erno Jablonka and Sally Pilcher. Is there someplace we can talk?" It didn't flatter me much that the woman wanted my trade as well.

She smiled a bad-girl smile. "Come with me, sweetie."

Janie Callahan led me to a small, grubby room in the rear of the building, her long red hair and her derriere swaying like ships in moderate seas. Air-Wick and cigarette smoke might've helped the smell. She plunked her rear end onto wrinkled sheets that neither smelled nor looked worth touching. "Talk?" she asked, undoing the top button of her sweater.

I took a wooden chair with most of its brown paint gone, hung my topcoat on the back, and sat. "Yeah, I'll ask questions about what happened yesterday, and you answer them. I'll pay for your time. Leave the buttons alone, sweetie."

The hooker giggled. "Ask away, muscles."

Janie told me she'd been sitting on the window ledge when "… this little half-frozen tub of lard waltzed in, hitch-hiking his thumb at me over his shoulder and calling out, 'How much for the beauty in the window?' Sally, the girl at the counter, took a break from sucking her boyfriend's tongue and told the fat man ten bucks, what we normally charge for a simple in-and-out job."

"The boyfriend being Erno Jablonka?" I took some notes.

Her act included a mocking grin.. "Two points for the cute guy! Yeah, that's the last I saw poor Erno alive. As for the chubby bastard, well, none of us ever seen him before. Well, the short fella says, 'Hey, at ten bucks a pop, I'll take two.' I tell him to follow me, and I'll round up another one." Janie danced another button out of its hole. Nothing but pale skin behind it.

"Is this where you took him?"

"Yeah, an' I told him I'd go grab another one while he got undressed. I told him I'd see who wanted to join us, an' I whipped off my sweater like this." She ripped it off as if it were a band-aid she no longer needed, and flipped it my way. I snatched it from the fetid air left-handed, not once letting my eyes wander from her magnetic breasts, telling myself to stay alert, and doing an excellent job of it.

The slogan for Lucky Strikes popped into my head—So round, so firm, so fully packed, so free and easy on the draw—but I didn't voice it. I met her green eyes and contrasted Scalzo's story with hers. "So, you got confused and thought the professor wanted sex with you and another woman?"

Her eyebrows shook hands. "No confusion about it, cutie. You're mixed up." She cupped her hands beneath the imposing breasts, gliding her thumbs over her nipples. "He called me a beauty. No doubt he wanted a jam session with me and another girl. What else can ya buy in a whorehouse? Campbell's soup? I went inta the hallway to see if Kayleigh—the skinny blonde you saw out front—or Sally's older sister, Veronica, wanted him. Minute later I thought I heard two shots."

"And—"

Janie stopped fiddling with her nipples, her face excited. "The fat man stood in the lobby when I caught up with him, a gun in his flabby mitt. I screamed, even before any of us spotted Erno and Sally dead on the floor. Half a minute a real cute cop runs in, pullin' out his pistol. Bags the killer and takes him away in cuffs when more cops show up. Most of us girls ran off by them."

I stood and threw the green sweater across her chest. "Kinda chilly in here, sweetheart," I noted. "You're nipples are poking out."

The hooker cocked her hips sideways as she wriggled into her sweater, swerving her chest and her Cheshire Cat grin the other direction.

I asked, "What happened then?"

"Well," she said, "Veronica Pilcher, Sally's older sister, ran out screechin' and falls onta Sally. Clever time to leave a whorehouse, with cops all around."

Out in the lobby, a trio of pistols waited.

"Somebody's in the wrong place," a bulky straw-haired babe with a small revolver sneered, slapping the barrel against her left hand. "Trespassing. We're jist gonna calm you down a little. Or a lot if we hafta."

"You don't hafta," I told her, more of a wise ass than I meant to be. "I'm just leaving." My .45, I remembered, was in the car. Good planning, Griffin.

———

"Dun't move, private dick."

The voice I heard behind me sounded deep, feminine, and Eastern European. "Dun't make me shoot you, snooper." Two or three sounds of footsteps, then the cocking of a pistol commanded my full attention. "I dun't need some dick annoying my staff wid a buncha stupid questions right after one of them got shot."

She walked around in front of me, a scratched-up pocket automatic in a black-gloved hand. I couldn't have said what she looked like. I only saw her pistol.

I froze, arms dangling. "I'm not armed, lady," I told her. "I'm not a threat to your operation here. And you don't need a third shooting in two days." Where have I seen this face?

"Also, dun't tell me what I cannot do. If I shoot you, we junk your body up in West Virginia mountains. You may know my name. I am Vera Dubchek, known as 'The Torch.' Dun't underestimate me, tough guy."

Criminy, the Torch. Her short brown hair looked gray in the newspapers, when? Maybe September. A jury acquitted her of racketeering and assault after a key witness disappeared. A tough woman in her forties, medium height, teeth clenched on a short cigarette wrapped in dark paper. She wore high heels and had the legs for them. "But I may have better uses for your body, toughie."

More footsteps, and a muzzle poked the back of my head. The mug behind me had a disturbing chuckle and a sweaty smell. Some of the hookers crowded through the doorway to the back room.

Time to go. "Well, hey," I said as casually as I could, "really great to meet you and the girls. I won't take up any more of your time. Bye." I scooted out, intact, in the luxurious freezing rain, and lived to tell the tale.

—

A block north of the no-name hotel, a smiling young cop tucked a ticket under a Chevy's wiper. I stopped next to him. "You the arresting officer in the double shooting yesterday?"

"The Torch's joint? Yeah. Jimmy Cochrane."

He ignored my I.D. I asked him to tell me about it, strolling back the way I'd come.

"See that hock shop up there?" He pointed. "As I passed it, I thought I heard maybe two small caliber shots. Started picking up my step and this little old hysterical lady in a gray coat runs around that corner and smack inta me, almost knocks me down. She yells, 'Somebody fired a gun,' and runs off. I'm there in three or four seconds or so, drawing my revolver and cocking it."

"And?"

"This short, squat creep is standing like he's waiting for a bus with an automatic that looks like a kid's cap pistol in his fat hand. Name of Scalzo. I almost shot him, grabbed the pistol's barrel and he let it go. Nobody else in the front till I spot these two pairs of feet as three hookers swarm in. I slapped cuffs on the whacko and called the precinct."

"Did you see Professor Scalzo fire a gun?"

"Well, actually, no. I was still around the corner when I heard him do it."

"Did you see Scalzo shoot anybody?"

"No. But he was holding a smoking pistol."

"That's it?"

"That's it."

As I turned to leave, a woman sang out, "Officer Cochrane, there you are!" We turned to look, and saw a tall, hefty woman with curly hair showing under a heavy crimson hat and coat. Her eyes locked on his, and she asked, "Have you seen that older lady, the kinda short one who ran around the corner screaming after the shots? I have something of hers."

Cochrane looked her over. "What, yesterday? Oh, I know which one you mean. I just mentioned her to this detective here."

She glanced my way, a serious type about fifty, and thrust a calf-gloved hand my way. "Hi, Detective. I'm Bridget Boyle. I teach art at Woodrow Wilson High School." They both seemed to think I was a police detective.

I shook her hand as she wiggled her middle finger in my palm. "Tell us about her, Bridget." A new witness?

"Sure. I headed to Chinatown for lunch with a friend, when I heard two shots just ahead of me. This older woman wearing a fur coat, shorter than I am, rushed out of the little building where the shooting took place. She called out something like, "He's shooting a gun,' and fled round the corner."

"That's when she bumped into me," Cochrane said. I nodded, taking notes.

The Boyle woman grabbed my arm. "Well, she bumped into me first, almost sent me flying. I threw out my arm and thought I caught it on her sleeve. She just ran. Turned out I'd snagged her bracelet, this gold one." The art teacher pulled a white handkerchief out of a coat pocket. "See? Real gold. The clasp broke and I wound up with it. The police questioned me at the scene, paying no attention to my reference to a lady dashing out the door and her jewelry."

She handed me the bracelet. Two items of interest. The open clasp had something reddish-brown on the open end, something dried on. And a bauble dangled from the middle, a half-inch plaque with "CM" engraved on it in elegant lettering.

I asked her a few more questions. Bridget described a well-dressed matron of perhaps sixty—brown hair streaked with gray, a pallid face, chocolate eyes, pudgy. "Attractive for her age, though," Boyle added, as I took her name and phone number. "Keep the bracelet," she said. "You're more likely to stumble across her than I am."

Settling into my car and heading for my office on Capitol Hill, I glanced at my watch. 1:33. I'd done all I could at the Torch's humpery for the time being. Frankly, I had little to show for it. The police and the hookers all supported the marginally credible tale that an unknown senior professor came to a shabby, unmarked brothel, chatted briefly with a hooker, then murdered another one and her boyfriend. Motive? Scalzo didn't seem like a homicidal nutcase.

Nobody but the Professor backed his looney alternate story. The Bible proved nothing at all, and his wife clearly believed he knew damned well the joint was a whorehouse. Two versions, both nutty as a tin roof sundae. But two people ended up dead. Maybe it's about them instead of Scalzo.

Deciding to ask Erno Jablonka's colleagues some questions, I rounded a few corners and headed for Georgetown, where the chauffer worked. The farther I drove from Mission Lane, the better the buildings looked, the cleaner the streets were swept, the fewer garbage cans lay battered by the curb. I stopped in front of 41 Ogden Park, the address I'd copied for Deputy Treasury Undersecretary Beauregard Bragg Madison and his wife—the dead man's employers— and slogged to the staff door in back. A clean-cut young man answered and invited me inside when I rang the bell. "My name is Cummings, sir," he said. "May I help you?"

We stood in a small hallway near the kitchen, a few other servants milling around, attracted to the doorbell like Republicans to paper money. The men wore dark suits, the women black uniform dresses trimmed in white lace. I spoke loudly: "Name's Griffin, private detective investigating the murder of Erno Jablonka."

Staff from across the room ventured closer, mumbling.

"Did Jablonka have any enemies?"

"That bastard," snarled a maid in the growing crowd, "he was a liar, a coward, a cheat and a thief. Even Madame Madison has been in a terrible mood since she learned yesterday—"

Cummings raised a cautionary hand. "Now, Colette, be careful. She'll—"

"What, Giles?" The accent was French, but not heavy. "Fire me and report me for stealing that never happened, like she did to the Irish girl? Have two of you men beat me, like poor Marie? No, I am quitting now."

"Colette's right." Another French maid, cropped black hair and a top-heavy figure. "After Derek, the garage man, spoke with Madame yesterday morning, she stormed out—well, drove into the snowstorm—in the Packard, shouting filthy words about firing Erno."

"Shouting?" I thought.

The maid leaned close to me and whispered. "If you came to interview for the job, Madame gave it to Derek last night, after auditioning men on staff." She giggled. "Madame knows what she wants from the men. Don't tell her I said so." Then she planted a little kiss on my cheek and stepped away from me.

An angry-looking woman strode down the staircase. I tagged her around sixty, with a brown bun and a thick waistline. She wore a low-cut nightgown of lavender silk with a matching bed jacket. Perhaps I'd interrupted a nap.

"I heard you from the stairs and I want you out of here immediately," she barked. "I have no need for a cheap shamus barging into my home and fomenting my staff to unruliness. You presumptuous bastard!" She spat in my direction.

"I gather you're Mrs. Madison," I said. "A couple of questions, if you don't mind."

"'If I don't mind!'" she yelled. "I told you to get out." When she strode over and slapped my face, I realized how much shorter than I she stood.

"Lady, I shot back, "this is the second time today I've been warned off this case by the madame of a whorehouse, claiming to care for her staff. I don't buy it."

She stormed into a small room, snatched a revolver out of a desk, and cocked it as she came back, while my hand stopped at the edge of my shoulder holster. I dropped my mitt and softened my voice. "Your name's Carolyn, isn't it?"

She cocked her head. "So what if it is?"

"Two ladies saw you at the brothel and picked up your initial bracelet." I waved it. "Your chauffer cheated on you, so you shot him and his girlfriend."

I slapped the gun out of her hands and the blonde maid called the cops. Secretary Madison bailed his wife out an hour later. The authorities dismissed the charges against her after four months for "insufficient evidence." They let Professor Scalzo go long before that. Hard to convict a jolly fat man who acts like Don Quixote and looks like Sancho Panza, and marches into a whorehouse to buy a *Bible*.

Don't Deny Yourself the Pleasure

Colin James

No trees have been destroyed during
the making of this hologram.
Let me walk you through it.
A side view of a hill
long incline without barriers.
The brain has its preferences.
Someone's handiwork like graffiti
without the object backers
just nicely hanging there.
We used to be able to get
atmospheric dry ice from the drugstore,
or was it the hardware man?
Don't know if it's an improvement.
The hills are alarmed by allegory
approaches, rebuffs, repetitions
defer to the crush of you.

Discontent in the Planet Props Dept

Colin James

I have been out of it for some time
holding this rope, impossible
to say exactly how long.
We have devised a set of signals.
If I get one tug on the rope
I pull Venus into declaratory orbit.
If I get two tugs Mars, etc.
Can't afford to daydream
but there are periods when I do.
Litter from the many Plastic Ono Experiments
have stuck to me, I am inconceivably imbued.
Don't want to stoop to killing time but
there are currently too many sunsets to choose.
Revising the old theory on threes and sevens,
my notes float in dead letter data mode.
Due for some time off if you count infinitude.

Students of the Subterranean

Colin James

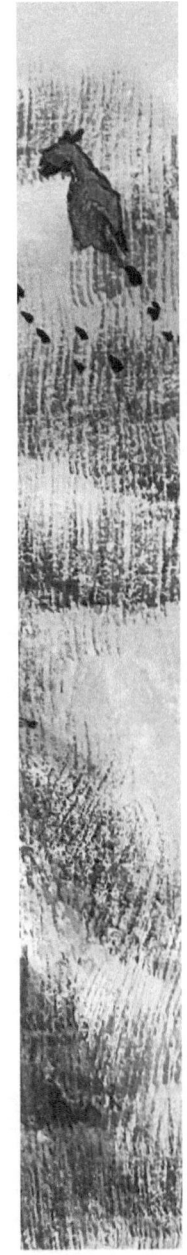

Stoically inept warnings
were posted all over the grounds.
We proceeded to take notice,
regarding our saintly Professor's
labyrinth course.
Centuries old oak and then
a postulant orifice.
Some stone steps, damp
moss imbued brick arches.
A crawl was negotiated
until a compromised posture
provided relief to extremities.
Guttural cynics transpired
to cough lifeless, angular despondency.
There was much throwing of antiquates
and authentication of The Narl.

The Visionary Company
William Doreski

Following bear tracks at dusk
I'm less than a mile from home
but the forest cramps like a muscle
and mist smokes from the dirty snow
and conceals me from myself.

I turn to retrace my boot prints
but they've disappeared. Figures
congeal in the watery gloom—
husky as Blake illustrations
but with muddled expressions.

The figures crumple as the mist
thickens and the light fades. Of course
they weren't really Los or Urizen
or other psychic malfunctions
but gauzy shadows woven

by the solstice to warn me
to get home before dark. I tromp
east and smell wood smoke curdling
from a metal stack. Emerging
from the woods, I observe my boot prints

sidling to the edge of the yard,
then returning. Have I stayed home
after all? I creep to the house,
peer in a window. There I am,
watching a football game, Patriots

versus the Jets, blue shirts and green.
I look so comfortable with teacup
and book in my lap. Returning
to the forest, I retrace the tracks
I didn't make but must be there.

If I look hard enough maybe
those shadows will become figures
again, and the crowd of us
will track the bear to its den
and cuddle up with it. Then winter

with a renewed sense of purpose
will expend itself in storms as drab
as the shades of gray we members
of the visionary company
wear for glory, not for warmth.

Sheltering in Ourselves
William Doreski

The wind is reshaping itself
to avoid fresh expectations.

Snow dishevels the scenery
that had planned a million flowers.

Only April, but already birds
have scouted their brittle estates,

already hundreds of chipmunks
have doggedly scoured the ground.

I'm happy to lie late in bed,
but you want to resurrect antique

flavors, boiling them on ranges
fueled by gas formed underground

before humans evolved. You want
to toss enormous salads

a brontosaurus might admire.
This reiteration of foodstuffs

reacts to a mid-spring snowstorm
as reagents respond to acids.

Such a descant of the spirit
usually occurs near the solstice,

when heat and thunder mingle
to thump out musical metaphors

as we shelter in ourselves.
Today's already awash in sighs.

The political news shocks us,
the bad actors lost in their roles.

The rise in sea level persists,
eroding properties that once
we coveted for long horizons.
Now we'd rather lose perspective

than see how the vanishing point
has cuddled up to our estate.

You're brewing potables that reek
of vinegar strong enough to kill

the most persistent microbes.
The morning looks too humble

to sustain our mutual worries,
so let's step outside in the snow

and wind and lie down and relax
in the season's last refurbishing.

Winter Weasel Afoot

William Doreski

A white bolt across the yard,
into the barn, around the barn,
into the coop, out with a mouse.

The weasel's faster than snow,
subtler than a farewell kiss,
bolder than a stroke of luck.

Already the day pardons itself,
tearing at its clothes, weeping.
That slain mouse emits a ghost

in exquisite gray tones people
like us envy. You note that
the weasel's winter outfit

is fluff as bright as a deer's.
I respect its appetite, honed
by cunning no human can match.

The weasel didn't rouse the hens
but savaged the mouse and ran
to a lair we haven't discovered.

You want to reinforce the coop,
fence it with warnings and threats,
but the weasel will find its way.

We've only three hens. Stash them
in the basement every night
until weasel season ends.

SOLSTICE

The days telescope and fade
so quickly they hardly seem real.
Christmas overstates itself

as usual, parking a blushing rump
on the village green and sighing
for the lost vicissitudes of youth.

The weasel punctures and punctuates
the solstice with tracks we could trace
across the frozen yellow marsh

to some ulterior landscape
where standard dogmas don't apply
and hunger always feels welcome.

Arctic Circle Sestina

Annie Percik

The sky alive with arcs of green-hued light;
They swirl and skirl as angels in the air.
The shifting colors show a changing face;
Like waterfalls the lights stream to the ground.
Night cries aloud the majesty of life;
In awe we gaze and sense that we are small.

The canopy of stars is full of small
Points of brightness shedding hazy light
On upturned faces. Moments in this life
Fade before the view. Up in the air
Heaven's light shines down and on the ground
People meet their maker face to face.

The light inspires people there to face
The insignificance of daily small
Aggravations. On the snowy ground
The stars seem far away and yet their light
Still reaches us through years of empty air
And promises the chance of other life.

By day the scene takes on a different life
Of blinding whiteness. Covering your face
Is vital to escape the chilling air.
The snow is endless. Footsteps need be small.
Trees cast pink and orange in the light
Appear as coral sprouting from the ground.

Strange tracks trail through the snow upon the ground,
Reminding me that ordinary life
Is very far away. The sunrise light

SOLSTICE

Shines green around the circle's flaming face,
The colors brighter though the time is small
That sunlight penetrates the icy air.

Silence reigns as nothing stirs the air,
Alone the thud of boots upon the ground.
Man-made sound disrupts the very small
But perfect chance of quiet in this life
Of bustle. Stop your noise and turn your face
Towards the arcing haze of wondrous light.

The green-hued light, the chill upon the air,
The upturned face, the snow thick on the ground.
The cherished life, the joy of moments small.

Desperately Seeking Spirit
Stephanie Cassatly

Deus est circulus cuius centrum est ubique, cuis circumferentia vero nusquam.
[God is a circle whose center is everywhere, but whose circumference is nowhere]
  —*Carl Jung, in "The Listener." January 21, 1960*

For my sixth birthday, my parents gave me a Magic Eight Ball, an inexpensive gift that captured hours of my attention, answering profoundly important questions such as, "Will George Wright (secretly nicknamed George Wrong) get in trouble for lifting my friend Jill's dress on the playground today?" Huddled together with a group of girlfriends, including my inquiring and humiliated friend, Jill, we sat spellbound, looking to this object as if it was a cosmic judge, able to settle world disputes with a single sentence. It provided utterly believable answers such as "Outlook good" or "Hazy, ask again later." Somehow, this little black plastic ball, full of liquid, with an answer cube that floated to the window whenever inverted, seemed to have all the answers for the endless scenarios and questions I could conjure.

By the time I was eight, the Magic Eight Ball, now buried in the back of a closet, was replaced by my Ouija Board, a stepped-up version of divining the future and communicating with other worlds. As we placed our fingers on the roaming planchette spelling out messages from beyond, my friends and I performed magical ceremonies and séances, often scaring ourselves half to death. My friend, Anne, conjured dead relatives and strangers as seamlessly as a teacher performing roll call. I never questioned her heavy hand on that planchette, which buzzed from letter to letter, revealing a shameless amount of information she already secretly knew.

In elementary school, playground time consisted of Chinese jump rope and a levitation game we called "Light as a Feather, Stiff as a Board." After after a quick incantation, four of my girlfriends could put a fifth friend, lying prostrate on the grass with arms crossed over chest like a mummy, into a trance-like or rapturous state, and then at the count of three, lift her up using just two fingers on each hand. For maximum goose bumps, especially used at sleepovers, we'd tell our prostrate friend to imagine her death, an out of body experience of sorts. On adrenaline alone, we probably could have lifted her and her mahogany coffin.

For as long as I remember, I was always attracted to the occult, the paranormal, the unexplained, unseen mysteries of the world. Certain they held the answers to the universe, I could never reconcile that certain truths might always remain unknowable.

Evidently, I wasn't the only person fascinated by the occult and paranormal because Rod Serling's 60s and 70s Hollywood hits, *The Twilight Zone* and *Night Gallery*, offered up almost two decades of thought provoking and chilling stimulus for curious people like me. Among the hundreds of episodes I watched transfixed, the one I remember most was "Little Girl Lost," where a man is awakened in the middle of the night by the cries of his daughter. When he enters her room, he finds that she has vanished, yet he can still hear her crying out for help, presumably from some other dimension. Suspended somewhere between fascinated and terrified, I experienced a transference of sorts, where I became that little girl, trapped and unable to return, imagining what this other place looked and felt like. Around this time, I began taking a running two-foot leap into my bed every night, for fear of some porthole or hatch door under my bed that would suck me into another dimension if my feet got too close to the edge.

It was this other dimension, albeit eerie, where things were unexpected and unexplained, that drew me in. Perhaps it fed some unconscious desire to break out of my known world, my structured life where things always seemed to fit logically together. My father, an engineer who worked for IBM, was an orderly and strict man. In his billfold, all the paper money faced the same way, same side up and in sequential order. His socks always had to be folded the same way and separated by color in his drawers. "An organized mind is a successful mind," he'd say. He was the captain of a well-run ship. The rest of my family, his crew, knew what was expected of us. My mother, the anchor, kept us moored with regular traditions and a steadfast heart.

All this time I was a good Catholic girl. My first Holy Communion, with white dress, gloves, patent leather shoes and a lace veil on my head, was an ethereal event. Taking that holy wafer into my mouth for the first time, as the body of Christ dissolved on my tongue and the incense wafted into my nose, eyes and lungs, I was infused with a sense of euphoria, as if every cell in my body had been cleansed. And then there was the wine, the forbidden fruit, of which I was allowed a small sip every week, consciously swishing and savoring the taste after the chalice touched my lips.

Up on the altar, Father Priestly (I swear that was his name), an elderly, disheveled Irishman, would murmur curses under his wine-infused breath as he fumbled with the prayer book trying to find his place. Evidently, he drank from the chalice before, during and after every mass. This was reported to me directly from a reliable source, my brother, the head altar boy. This happened almost every Sunday and was the first and only time I ever heard of a priest saying "goddammit." Father Priestly also came to our home for dinner occasionally, as it was the tradition of our tight knit expatriate community to take turns hosting him every Sunday night. The Monday morning scuttlebutt was always how we had to drive him home and put him to bed.

In addition to communion, I went to confession regularly, spilling out my infractions through the thin screen between me and God's henchman: "Last week I told my brother's girlfriend he had diarrhea after the first time he asked her out," or "I've been sitting in my bathroom every night reading my friend's older brother's *Playboy* magazine with the shower on, so my parents think I shower every day."

I went on religious retreats, attended mass weekly and played my guitar while singing and swaying to Kumbaya with the church folk group. Being Catholic was like an old pair of pajamas. There was comfort in these familiar rituals, and a curiosity of sorts, especially the part about the Holy Spirit.

With all those Catholic hymns, prayers and rituals etched like cave drawings on the inside of my skull, I did, however, wonder if I was going to burn in hell for exploring the occult, or what was considered by some to be blasphemy or the dark side. Was I living a double life? My first clue of this inner controversy had come much earlier, when the mother of one of my good Catholic friends forbade her to play with the Ouija board at my house. "Why?" I asked. "Because she says we're flirting with the Devil." I had seen *The Omen*, which resulted in my sleeping with a rosary around my neck and a Bible on my chest for weeks afterward. Courting the Devil or any evil spirits was the last thing I wanted to do, but my curiosity was a force to contend with.

In my teens, my interest in metaphysics shifted to books. Reading *The Reincarnation of Peter Proud* and then various books on the life of Edgar Cayce launched me into a whole new realm of curiosity, fueling my secret desire to become a psychic, as if it were as easy as tuning into the right radio frequency. I tried meditating, hoping to receive messages from beyond, squinting, which glazed my vision enough to think I could see auras, sleeping with pen and paper in hand in case something came to me in a dream or from the spirit world (aka automatic writing in psychic lingo). Brian Weiss's work in *Many Lives, Many Masters* and James VanPragh's *Talking to Heaven* cinched it for me. I wanted to unlock my subconscious, communicate with deceased relatives, learn who I was in past lives, and perhaps even get to know a few of my old selves a little better.

There seemed to be an invisible line between the acceptable and unacceptable, the good and the bad, the religious and the occult. Yet, wasn't Edgar Cayce a good Christian as well as a psychic? He was a Bible-toting Sunday school teacher who went into deep trances, receiving messages from beyond and enabling him to diagnose and cure hundreds of strangers' illnesses as well as regress himself into their past lives. And what about St. Theresa De Avila and Thomas Aquinas? They were known to have levitated for hours at a time during ecstatic experiences. There seemed to be plenty of mysticism in Christianity.

I wanted to understand everything possible from the mystical world, without giving up or abandoning my Christian roots. Wasn't all this ultimately heading in the same direction? Surely, I wasn't doing anything wrong. Or was I? Such was the Catholic gift of guilt. Thankfully, a former Catholic nun once reassured me, "Guilt is simply your ego tricking you into thinking you're making moral progress. Don't fall for it." Despite this though, I still felt betwixt and between.

Although I was born a few years too late to call myself a flower child, I rode the coattails of that era in college, over a decade later, in the 70s. I trailed The Grateful Dead with my friends, dancing unabashedly, twirling under the misty moonlight and under the influence of magic mushrooms, while still looking for the meaning of it all. However, the sudden and untimely death of my mother, a homicide in the middle of my freshman year, jerked me into an entirely different reality. Like being blindfolded and dropped off a train in the middle of nowhere, with no map or ticket to go home, my disorientation was profound. In addition to my sense of bottomless sorrow, her death fueled a deep confusion and desperate ache for understanding, a seemingly hopeless endeavor. I can still clearly conjure that highly charged night when, in the middle of *It Must Have Been the Roses*, the dike broke, and tears spilled forth like a gushing river. I felt the full magnitude of her death, and then only moments later, as if I had finally expelled all of my grief, I began to laugh uncontrollably, until my stomach ached. Wondering at first if I had lost my mind, I finally thought I understood the truth—that joy and sorrow can co-exist equally. If only it could have been that simple. While Jerry Garcia's guru status offered some semblance of an embrace that night, the cold and hollow anticlimax of the next day, and many more like it, left me dangerously hanging by a thread.

On a frigid January night in Raleigh, North Carolina, a year after my mother had been killed, leaving one too many concerts with my Dead Head friends, we drove up an exit ramp of a highway, going the wrong way into oncoming traffic. Through the thick fog of our minds, we couldn't connect the dots. The oncoming headlights of a brilliant eighteen-wheel semi-truck, perhaps misinterpreted as the light of truth we were seeking, swerved away from us onto the shoulder, narrowly missing us within a hair of our lives. As if some invisible reins pulled me to back to safety, the next day I bid farewell to my Dead Head friends, who continued on to the next concert, and boarded a Greyhound bus back to school.

I took a hiatus from meandering in the mystical during my twenties, my post-college and early career years. I was too busy trying to pay the rent and car insurance, not to mention eat one square meal a day. My curious spirit turned to winter, and I was blanketed by the sobriety of two realities, my mother's meaningless death and the uncertain future that lay ahead. I needed to stand on my own two feet, to make a living, to become an adult, to find my way.

Like the groundhog emerging to see his shadow after a long hibernation, a question of faith surfaced slightly when I met my husband to be. Raised in different faiths, we were forced to consider in what church, if any, we would marry. What faith, if any, we would follow. I was surprised to realize how important it was to me that we have a Catholic wedding, how deep my roots really went. My husband, an agreeable man for the most part, conceded. But like the groundhog not quite ready to usher in Spring, after the wedding I returned to my hole, continuing my hiatus until becoming a mother myself.

Following the birth of two daughters in my early thirties, my old curiosity rekindled. It was a newer, more updated version, though. As if the miracle of giving birth and my fierce new love had closed one door and opened another, I unknowingly crossed an invisible line. The best way I can think of it was a shift from the mystical to the spiritual. Yet the two seemed so related, like siblings of different ages. Where the mystical dealt with mysteries that transcended ordinary human knowledge, the spiritual seemed to deal with the same, and also ascribe to some higher, omnipotent source.

With every illness, accident or field trip away from home, my silent prayers for my children became mantras of, "Please, God, keep them healthy and safe." When I read or heard about a mother dying, it was, "Please, God, let me live to see them grow." My worries seemed too big for me to carry alone. Relinquishing part of it to a higher power made it bearable somehow.

Despite our different backgrounds, my husband and I wanted to find a mutually agreeable faith community in which to raise our daughters. It was "church du jour" for a while, until we finally settled on the Episcopal church, a comfortable bridge between Catholic and Eastern Orthodox, where we connected with a number of young families and a strong sense of community. I established a meaningful relationship with one of the pastors (a divorced lesbian with a tattoo on her ankle – a far cry from Father Priestly). We joked about how many Catholics became Episcopalians; she called herself a "recovering Catholic." It was in this church, with this unconventional pastor, that I found a way to forgive my mother's killer, a transformative event that unburdened me in ways I could never have imagined. After serving twenty years of his life sentence for the crime he committed, I found her killer just before he died in Angola State Penitentiary. In forgiving him, I realized I had been just as much of a prisoner.

In my late thirties, I joined a reading group with twelve fabulous women from all walks of life. At one meeting, after reading a more spiritual book, I was speaking with my Indian friend, Bubli, a Buddhist who meditates for over an hour every day and has her very own yogi. "You're a seeker, Steph," she said to me. I was strangely open to her remark. Previously in my life, I might have been offended, feeling as though it were a condemnation about being unsure of myself, a weakness of sorts. But there was an undeniable truth and perhaps even a subtle compliment in what she said. Seekers are curious and not necessarily lost.

I began reading more and more about seekers, both fictional and non-fictional. St. Augustine, the ultimate seeker, in his "Confessions," spent much of his life "betwixt and between," until he had his archetypal epiphany under a fig tree. And even then, he wasn't a serene convert. He went kicking and screaming all the way to sainthood. More than a few times in history, this story has been repeated. Didn't Gandhi, Mohammed and Christ all seek to connect with the divine? Didn't they just have different words and rituals for the same goal? Don't all roads lead to Rome?

Now, beyond adulthood and well into middle age, where I'm questionably wiser and more mature, seeking the meaning of life and who is in charge seems to have morphed into a simple desire for grace and peace, like two friends I really want to get to know better. Grace is the one who always takes the high road, avoiding nasty retorts like, "I told you so." Peace is the calm one who doesn't get rattled and finds a way to forgive, even the gravest of injustices. I also seek to ditch a third friend, my lifelong companion and stalker, "Worry." What good has she been to me? She's dragged me down and wasted far too much of my time. I'm drawn to inner serenity that comes with trust, with believing in my bones, that something much bigger than me is in control. Although still a back seat driver, I have become more adept at surrendering the wheel.

And what of raising my daughters to be spiritual beings? I believe I have an unspoken responsibility to offer something up to them. When they've occasionally asked questions like, "What is heaven?" or "Who is God?" I've tried to answer, sometimes meandering until they finally lose interest. In four decades, from Magic Eight Ball to Grace and Peace, I still don't have perfect answers, but spirituality is a nebulous and grounding gift I'm trying to give them before they wander out into the world.

In between yoga classes, meditation and occasional church, I am like a heat seeking missile; I keep moving toward the warmth, toward what calls me home. But now I'm less interested in hitting the target than I am in the journey itself. Actually, the journey has become the target and I feel comfortable and somewhere near the center of it.

Where once I twirled under the misty moon, feeling so dizzy I didn't know which way was up, I have come to feel my feet planted more firmly on the earth. I recently shared one of my essays with a relative; it was about finally finding closure two decades after my mother's death. She wrote me later and said, "I hope you realize God's hand has been on your shoulder all along." With more equanimity than ever before, I responded, "I do!"

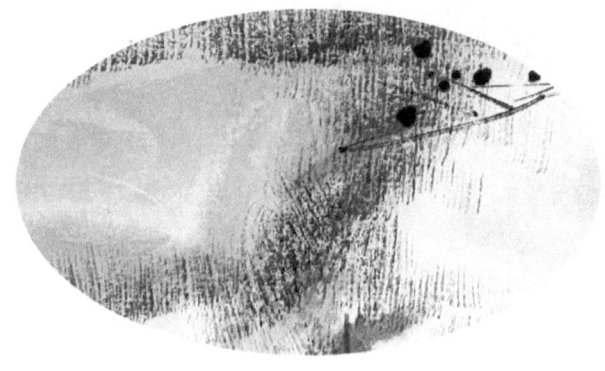

Coda
Morgan Golladay

It began with the light rush,
and breaking and flooding
of words and sounds,
all articulating the madness
of creative energy exploding into being.
As light became form,
as sound moved mountains,
so the soul of the universe
moderated itself
into itself
and became a unity.

At the end of my days
I wonder at it all,
seeing the beginning,
sensing the ending,
caught in a dreamtime
of waiting
for the next rush of light.

Chocolate Chip Pancakes
Christian Fitzgerald

Mom hovers over my bed; it's pitch black, and I'm confused. She's said something. "What?," I say.

"Paul's mom called and asked if we could help her out before school. Get up, we're taking Paul to breakfast."

I prop myself up on my arm and rub sleep from my eyes. "What time is it?"

Already out of the room and bustling around, she calls back. "It's early."

The blurry red numbers on my desk clock say 4:58. "What?" I say again, mostly to myself. "Paul?"

Moments later I'm bundled in my new winter coat, boots, hat and gloves. We step out the front door. Immediately wind whips snow into our faces pushing us back. Drifts of snow have piled up on the porch against the house. We crunch through it to the car. "Geez mom, it's still nighttime."

"Honey, when someone needs help, we help."

"Yeah but I haven't been friends with Paul since fourth grade."

"It doesn't matter."

Somehow the leather seat in the car feels colder than the wind outside. I watch mom scrape snow and ice from the windshield as the car struggles to warm up. Our Christmas lights blink red like warning lights through the frosted window. She climbs in and backs out of the driveway.

"Can't his mom just drop him at our house or something? We could watch TV until school. I don't want to go to breakfast with him."

She ends the conversation with, "This is happening."

Still freezing, I huddle up and look out the window. We turn out of our subdivision. There's no one out on the road except a plow noisily scraping snow to the side. Through living room windows, people's

Christmas trees sparkle dreamily, making me wish I was back in my warm bed. We turn on to Main Street, pass convenience stores and smoke shops and a tattoo parlor. At the self-storage center, we turn onto Paul's street and the car bumps over railroad tracks. His house is one in a long row of single-story brick duplexes. Faded plastic toys and bikes with training wheels poke out of the snow in front yards. We pull up in front of Paul's house; it's smaller and more ragged than I remember. Paul sits in the dark on the front stoop, flanked by rusty wrought iron rails. He stands and approaches us. He's wearing beat up black sneakers, black jeans, and a black hoodie pulled tight, no gloves or coat. He looks thin and cold. I sigh. This is going to suck.

"Thanks, Mrs. Brody." He says as he slides in next to me. He smells... not dirty, but dusty. Like a cardboard box that's been in the basement for a long time.

"It's no problem, Paul," she says.

"Hey," he says, without making eye contact with me. He's fidgety and awkward as he buckles his seatbelt.

"Hey," I say back. It's the most we've spoken in at least a year.

Mom turns into the parking lot of the diner down the street from our high school. It's the only place that's open. Garland and colorful lights dress the windows, and a small, artificial tree sits in the entryway, brightly decorated. The bell dings as we walk in. It's warm and welcoming. A few other groups of people huddle over coffee and breakfast.

A voice calls out to us, "Happy winter solstice!" A young waitress appears from the back. "First day of winter, the days only get longer from here." She's way too cheery for so early in the morning. "Sit where you like, I'll come take your order in a minute."

We get settled into a booth, mom on the inside, me next to her. Paul sits across from me.

Menus are tucked behind the salt, pepper, ketchup and syrup. Mom passes them out. "Get whatever you like, Paul."

"Ok, Mrs. Brody."

We're quiet as we make our choices. Cheery comes over. Somehow I knew what Paul was going to order: chocolate chip pancakes and chocolate milk. I get eggs over-easy, hash browns, and toast with orange juice. Mom just gets coffee. Cheery leaves, and Mom pulls out her laptop, getting a head start on work.

Paul looks up at me for the first time. "Winter solstice, huh?" he says.

"Yeah, how about that?" In my mind I'm rolling my eyes. Paul was always a little awkward and weird.

After a moment he says, "It's our anniversary."

"What?"

"You know, we became friends on the winter solstice."

I think back to that day. We were in the same class, but never played together. Then the last day of school before Christmas break I cut in front of him in line, so he punched me in the back of the head. It didn't hurt, but we got sent to the principal's office. It turned out that both of us had Snorlax as our favorite Pokémon, and we both loved pizza, and I guess at that age that was enough. We spent every moment of that Christmas break together, and most weekends after.

"Huh, so like nine years ago?

"It was kindergarten. Ten years."

He knows exactly how long we've been friends? Nothing creepy about that.

Cheery arrives with our food, and I tuck in. Mom doctors her coffee and is back to her email.

Paul seems to relax a little, and smiles. "Hey, remember when we found that toad in the woods behind my house?"

"Yeah, you wanted to keep it as a pet."

He laughs, "We got a shoe box for it, and we brought it to school."

A vivid image pops in my head of Paul and I digging in the mud by the little creek, exploring, looking for treasure, and finding that toad. I stayed to keep an eye on it while he went and got the shoebox. It took us awhile to scoop it into the box, but we were determined.

I smile, "Yeah, after that, Mrs. Jensen separated us."

"She sure did. Toady escaped from my backpack."

"Did we really name him Toady?" I ask.

He laughs again, warm and rich. The sound of it tugs on a nostalgia deep within me.

"I guess that's the best we could think of," he says.

We reminisce more, and I feel myself loosen up. I had forgotten how much fun we had together. Our conversation gets more and more animated, and at some point Mom looks up and smiles at us.

The bell dings and a woman swirls in from the cold. She approaches us. She's tattooed and seems like she's in her late twenties, until she gets closer, and I can see the creases around her eyes and mouth.

"Paul, let's go."

Suddenly she's next to our table. The cold from outside pours off her and she smells like stale cigarettes.

"Oh, hi Aunt Dee."

She folds her arms. "Yeah, hi. Come on, let's go."

Mom starts to introduce herself, but it seems like Aunt Dee wants none of it. Before Mom has a chance to say anything, Aunt Dee says, "Hurry up, I'll be in the car." She leaves, the bell dinging behind her.

Mom says, "Well, it was nice to see you again, Paul."

"You too, Mrs. Brody. Thanks for breakfast."

"Of course."

Paul stands and lingers by the side of the table for a moment.

"See you at school," I say.

"Uh, about that. I'm going to live with Aunt Dee, so I won't be back at school."

"Oh," I say, surprised, and sad, and guilty all at once.

He leans down and gives me an awkward hug, trapping my arms. When he stands, his eyes glisten. "You've been a good friend."

I'm at a loss for words, but then he's leaving and the ding of the bell is ringing through my head.

Across the table from me sits his plate, his pancakes untouched, next to a full glass of chocolate milk.

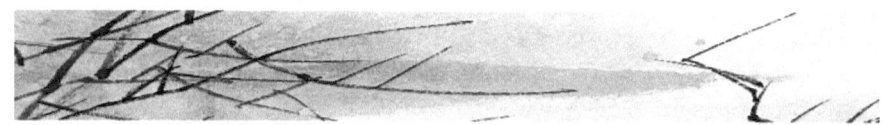

All the Leaves are Brown

Gabby Gilliam

Does the insect
        protest the swing
of seasons—the drop
        in the stomach
when temperatures plummet
        before the rising arc
of Spring awakening
           or does it embrace

dormancy—yearn

        for the sluggish sunrise

expanding night

        the frigid freeze

           that forces it to grow still?

Winter Wardrobe

Gabby Gilliam

Heads of auburn
and chestnut brown
shake themselves bald

fallen leaves scattering
to collect in storm drains
snag on windshield wipers

crunch beneath feet
bare branches stretch
expectantly—awaiting

a fresh coat of virgin snow
ready to shiver and doze
beneath the soft white winter.

At Least Our Hearts Were Warm

Gabby Gilliam

Sharp sound of blades on ice slices through still winter night. We skate in circles beneath artificial lights which do nothing to keep the chill at bay.

Distant stars above
twinkle, muted by our lights.
Ancient spectators.

The surface slushes as we grate a track around the wall. Timid skaters hug the edge, have dampened knees from their battle against their balance.

They become a blur
as we speed past, our laughter
bouncing on the ice.

The lights click off one by one—a subtle sign that it's time to leave. We seek hot chocolate to warm our hands and throats; let its steam thaw lips and noses.

No one is ready
to relinquish this perfect
night beneath the stars.

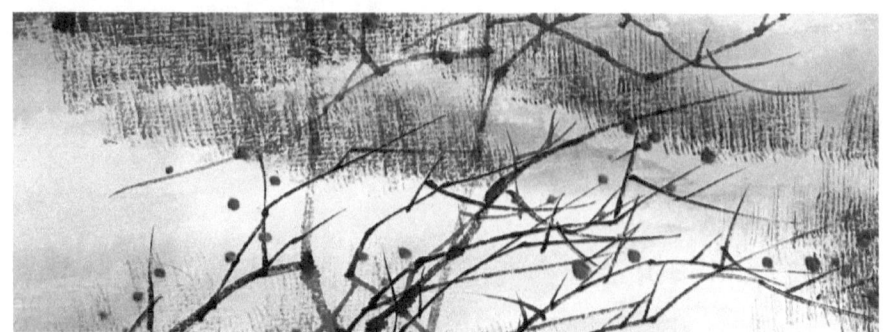

Contributor Bios

AAKAASH

Buffy Aakaash grew up around hills and lakes in New Jersey west of New York City. He has lived as a queer man in both big cities and small remote towns throughout the US since then —backwoods Tennessee, Seattle, New York, San Francisco, high desert New Mexico, not in that order, but finally New England. His poetry has been published in *The Poet Magazine*, *Iris Literary Journal*, *The Write Launch*, *Main Street Rag*, *The Raven's Perch*, *Dissonance Magazine*, *Oberon*, Sweety Cat Press, and others.

Untangling the Knots, his chapbook "hot to" poems, will be published by Kelsay Books in December of 2022.

With years of experience living in intentional communities, a community builder at heart, he recently settled into life in the Green Mountains of Central Vermont, with his dear canine companion, Bodhi.

More at buffyaakaashpoetry.com

APRILL

Lynn Aprill is an award-winning poet and educator whose work has appeared recently or is forthcoming in *Creative Wisconsin* magazine, *Copperfield Review Quarterly*, *Bramble*, *Wingless Dreamer*, *Quartet Journal*, *Willows Wept Review*, *Ekphrastic Review* and others.

A Wisconsin native, she received a BA in English from UW-Eau Claire and an MA in Curriculum and Instruction from UW-Milwaukee. Her poem "Love" was recently selected as the 3rd-place winner in the 73rd annual Jade Ring Writing Contest of the Wisconsin Writers Association. *Channeling Matriarchs*, her first chapbook with Finishing Line Press, was published in August 2021. She resides with her husband and various dogs on 40 acres in Northeast Wisconsin.

More at lynnaprill.weebly.com

BERN

Alan Bern is a retired children's librarian and cofounder with artist/printer Robert Woods of the fine press/publisher Lines & Faces (linesandfaces.com). Alan has a hybrid (poetry, prose, and photos) fictionalized memoir forthcoming from *Uncollected Press* and is the author of three books of poetry.

He is a Pushcart Prize nominee, and recent awards include Honorable Mention for Free Verse in SouthWest Writers Annual Writing Contest, *A Diversity of Expression* (2022); Honorable Mention for Littoral Press Poetry Prize (2021); Flash Fiction Finalist for "Ekphrastic Sex" (2021); First Runner-up for Raw Art Review's Mirabai Prize for Poetry (2020); a Medal from SouthWest Writers for a WWII story set in Assisi (2019). Recent and upcoming writing and photo work: Haunted Waters Press, *Aletheia Literary Quarterly*, *Cerasus, Feral, The Hyacinth Review*, Reunion: *The Dallas Review*, and *Mercurius*. Alan performs with dancer/choreographer Lucinda Weaver as Paces: dance and poetry fit to the space and with musicians from Composing Together.

CASSATLY

Stephanie Cassatly is the author of *Notice of Release: A Daughter's Journey to Forgive Her Mother's Killer* (eLectio Publishing, 2017). Her memoir received the Nautilus Book Award and has led her to speak publicly both nationally and internationally on the topic of forgiveness and restorative justice. She is also a contributor to The Forgiveness Project, an international nonprofit storytelling project that chronicles individual narratives and explores the boundaries, possibilities and universal nature of forgiveness. Her shorter works have appeared in various journals and anthologies.

In her spare time, she facilitates community-based workshops including after school teen creative journaling groups, resume writing and job interview coaching for recently released incarcerated and homeless individuals. Previously, she has taught writing at Palm Beach Atlantic University and Endicott College.

Stephanie holds a bachelor's degree in business from Emory University and a master's in writing from Vermont College of Fine Arts. She resides with her husband in Florida. Together they have two grown daughters.

More at stephaniecassatly.com

CLAYPOOL

After growing up in Missouri and then making Colorado her home for 20 years as she traveled the country as a consultant, Maggie Claypool now lives in the First State (Delaware) with her two rescue dogs, "Fancy" and "Chico." In her stories, she attempts to strike a resonant chord of emotion in the reader.

Her short stories have appeared in *Instant Noodles* Vol. 1 No. 3 ("The Gravy Boat"), *Spillwords* ("Watch Me"), *FromOneLine* Vol. 3 ("Well It's Done Now"), *Close to the Bone* ("Relative Secrets"), Instant Noodles Vol. 2, No. 1 ("Miss Luna's Visit"), and *The Dark City* Vol. 8 No. 1 ("The Motive"). She also regularly includes brief fiction in the blog on her website.

More at maggieclaypool.com

CRANDELL

William F. Crandell is a Vietnam Veteran. Fighting a dirty war as a rifle platoon leader and then marching for peace afterward gave him a bone-deep understanding of why honor and integrity are life-and-death concerns. Crandell returned home from Vietnam with a zest for adventure, a skeptic's eye, and a hundred thousand stories. He quickly acquired both an FBI file of his own and a doctorate in American history, but oddly enough, it was the years of spiritual retreat in the mountains that set his infantryman's feet back on solid ground. The writing came naturally–he'd been a foreign correspondent for an Ohio newspaper before college, and wrote fiction to stay awake in some of the jobs he held. Still, the years on Capitol Hill and in Federal law enforcement agencies gave him a player's knowledge of how crime and power operate, along with an appreciation of the dedication and the slime beneath the skin of America's capital. Awarded a Maryland State Arts Council Individual Artist Award for his private detective novel, *Let's Say Jack Kennedy Killed the Girl* (Hawkshaw Press), Crandell has published short stories, book reviews, scholarly articles, journalism, state and federal reports, political analyses, and congressional testimony that he presented in Washington hearings. Crandell's short story, "The Last Lootenant Wins His Fuckin' Medal," was awarded 1st Place (Short Stories, Single Story) by the NFPW in 2020.

An Ohio native, Crandell received all his degrees at Ohio State University, completing his doctorate in American History with a study of the interaction of McCarthyism and Republican politics. After "The Faith-Based Diet" won PRIZM's Mark Twain Award for

Humor/Social Commentary in 2012, Crandell and his writer wife, Judith Speizer Crandell, relocated to Delaware so they could write at the ocean's edge.

DECICCO

Kim DeCicco was born and raised in New York, where she earned a degree in history and a master's in museum studies. After moving to Delaware in 2004, she followed her dream of learning the craft of writing and was honored to receive the 2020 Delaware Division of the Arts Fellowship for Emerging Artist in Fiction. Since then, she has had stories published in the Rehoboth Beach Reads series (*Beach Secrets* and *Beach Dreams*) and in *Halloween Party '21* (Gravelight Press). When not writing, Kim spends her time peddling antiques and spoiling her ginger cat, Phoenix.

DORESKI

William Doreski lives in Peterborough, New Hampshire. He has taught at several colleges and universities. His most recent book of poetry is *Dogs Don't Care* (2022). His essays, poetry, fiction, and reviews have appeared in various journals.

DOYLE

Born and raised in Ireland, but resident in Brazil since 2000, Anthony Doyle works as a translator of fiction and nonfiction from Portuguese. He is the author of the children's book, *O Lago Secou*, and the forthcoming novel, *Hibernaculum* (Out Of This World Press, 2023). His short stories "Sam Bakki" and "Shark Fishing" were published in the summer 2021 issue of *Instant Noodles*, and "Shark Fishing" was a Pushcart Prize and Best of the Net nominee. Translated works include the novel *There Were Many Horses*, by Luiz Ruffato, and the nonfiction books *Rio de Janeiro: Extreme City*, by Luiz Eduardo Soares, and *Ideas to Postpone the End of the World*, by indigenous leader Ailton Krenak.

More at anthony-doyle.com

FITZGERALD

Christian Fitzgerald writes mostly science-fiction stories from the coast of North Carolina. He graduated from Berklee College of Music in Boston with a degree in Film Scoring, and has written music for an iPad app version of Jamie Lee Curtis's children's book, *Where Do Balloons Go?*, as well as the sitcom pilot *Brooklyn Shakara*, starring

Gbenga Akkinagbe of *The Wire*. When not writing stories, he writes songs on his acoustic guitar for his wife and three sons. They mostly love it.

More at christianfitzgerald.net.

FITZGERALD

Jane Fitzgerald is a retired history teacher and poet. She writes with clarity, compassion and insight. Jane has been passionate about poetry for over thirty years since she studied with David Ignatow at Columbia University where she earned a MA Degree. She has written four books including, *Notes From the Undaunted*. Her poetry has been featured in: *Your Daily Poem, Open Door Magazine, Dreamers Creative Writing, Sad Girls Club, Quillkeepers Press, Isele Magazine*, and more. Jane is a repeat poet for the Devil's Party Press.

She worked as a teacher in different types of situations from public schools in low-income areas to private schools. Jane hopes that others will find comfort and a sense of togetherness through her poetry. She grew up near New York City, but now lives in the sunny, diverse state of Florida.

More at facebook.com/janespoetry

FLEMING

Robert Fleming lives in Lewes, DE. His work has been published in United States, Canada, England, Ireland, and Australia. He is a member of the Rehoboth Beach and Horror Writer's Association. Awards and nominations: 2022 winner of San Gabriel Valley, CA, broadside-1 poem; 2021 winner of Best of Mad Swirl poetry; a double nomination for the Pushcart Prize and Best of the Net.

More at facebook.com/robert.fleming.5030

FULCHER

R. David Fulcher is an author of horror, science fiction, fantasy, and poetry. Major literary influences include H.P. Lovecraft, Dean Koontz, Edgar Allen Poe, Fritz Lieber, and Stephen King. Fulcher is the author of *Trains to Nowhere*, a historical drama set in World War II, and *Blood Spiders and Dark Moon*, a collection of fantasy and science fiction short stories (authorhouse.com). Fulcher's work has appeared in numerous small press publications including *Lovecraft's Mystery Magazine, Black Satellite, The Martian Wave, Burning Sky, Shadowlands, Twilight Showcase,*

Heliocentric Net, Gateways, Weird Times, Freaky Frights and the anthologies *Dimensions* and *Silken Ropes.*

Fulcher's work can also be found in the Gravelight Press collection, *Halloween Party 2019.* A passion for the written word has also inspired Fulcher to edit and publish the literary magazine, *Samsara* (samsaramagazine.net), which has showcased writers and poets for over a decade. Fulcher resides in Ashburn, Virginia, with his wife Lisa, and their rambunctious cats.

GILLIAM

Gabby Gilliam lives in the Washington, DC, metro area with her husband and son. Her poetry has most recently appeared in *Tofu Ink, The Ekphrastic Review, Pure Slush, Deep Overstock, Vermillion, MacQueen's Quinterly,* and *Equinox.*

More at gabbygilliam.squarespace.com

GOLLADAY

Morgan Golladay has been intrigued with words all her life. Her poetry reflects this, and she uses illusion and allusion in her writing.

Much of her work focuses on her native Shenandoah Valley, as well as coastal Delaware. Morgan says that poetry originated as an oral form, and she thinks it works best when it is heard. To that end it must be concise, simple, and tight. The poet bears the responsibility to speak old truths in new ways, to encourage the reader/listener to consider ideas from a different point of view. To do this the poet must be vulnerable, must allow their inner thoughts and fears and secrets to surface. This is particularly difficult in a society that doesn't share its hurts, its fears, its pain. And that poetry, of love, loss, sadness, fear, and joy binds us together in our humanity and give us opportunities to grow.

Morgan has worked with non-profits as a volunteer and staff, been a librarian, a blood donor recruiter, and a customer service and purchasing agent for a residential water-well wholesaler.

Her watercolor and acrylic-collage paintings have won awards, and she is a member of the Mispillion Art League in Milford, DE, where she currently lives. An emerging poet, her work has been published in the *Broadkill Review, Halloween Party '21,* and *Instant Noodles.* She is currently editing her first novel.

GONZALEZ

Bri Gonzalez (she/they) is a Chicana/e, queer poet from San Antonio, Texas. They're currently holed up and winter-bewitched in Colorado, receiving their MFA from the University of Colorado Boulder.

Her work can be found or forthcoming in *Brazos River Review, Janus Literary, Juke Joint, Coffin Bell,* ERGI Press, and more. In their free time, they enjoy bothering their void cat, Dahlia, binge-watching creature features, and fighting to keep their D&D characters alive.

More at bgwriting.org

JAMES

Colin James is the author of two chapbooks of poetry: *Dreams Of The Really Annoying* (Writing Knights Press) and *A Thoroughness Not Deprived of Absurdity* (Piski's Porch Press), and a book of poems, *Resisting Probability* (Sagging Meniscus Press).

JOHNSON

John Johnson is the rare poet who loves language but also data and numbers. He resides in Northern Virginia where, in addition to running a consulting firm as a professional econometrician, he loves pizza, professional wrestling, and regularly writes with his wild writing circle. Johnson's poetry tends to focus on humorous aspects of his geeky childhood and his journey as it relates to entrepreneurship, family and friendship, and failed athletic endeavors.

He is the author of two recently published chapbooks: *In the Mind of the Anxious Traveler* (Kelsay Books) and *Chalk Dust Memories* (Plan B Press).

More at poemsovercoffee.com

PERCIK

Annie Percik lives in London, writing novels and short stories, while working as a freelance editor. She writes a blog about writing on her website, which is where all her current publications are listed, including her novels, *The Defiant Spark* and *A Spectrum of Heroes*. You can also find information there about the media review podcast she co-hosts, and the photo-story blog recording the adventures of her teddy bear. He is much more popular online than she is.
More at alobear.co.uk

ROMEO

Between her career as a therapeutic personal chef, and maintaining the title of "King Baby's FUN mamma," Mary Beth Romeo gets strange in the wee hours of morning as she method acts the amnesiac gods of her queer fantasy manuscript.

Writing has always been "the one that got away" for MB, and she has finally reconnected with that first true love. But life has not been a total bust for creative flings. MB has a charming wife that likes to quote her scrapped dialogue, a master's degree in Urban Affairs, fifteen years served in social justice and community organizing, and past side hustles in illustration, ethically-questionable academic paper writing, and creative portrait photography.

As the middle of seven children from a poor-class NY family, where all parents tended toward crazy, MB gets much of her inspiration and dark humor from her chaotic upbringing and six quirky sibs. Oh. And when she talks about herself in the third person, it's always MB—but she digs the irony of her name on a girl who looks like a boy.

SALOME

Mary Salome (she/her) is an Arab- and Irish-American Buddhist, writer, and media activist who lives in San Francisco. She has produced radio, video, and web publications, and is currently a Digital Communications Supervisor at the University of California San Francisco. Her prose and poetry publications include *Food for our Grandmothers: Writings by Arab-American and Arab-Canadian Feminists, Tiny Seed Journal*, and *Archive of the Odd*.
More at twitter @marysalome

SHORT

Lisa Short is a Texas-born, Kansas-bred writer of fantasy, science fiction and horror. She has an honorable discharge from the United States Army, a degree in chemical engineering, and twenty years' experience as a professional engineer. Lisa currently lives in Maryland with her husband, youngest child, father-in-law and cats. She is a member of both SFWA and HWA.

More at facebook.com/lisashortwrites

VALENTINO

Katharine Valentino worked for thirty years at menial jobs before acquiring a BA degree—summa cum laude!—from Indiana University in Bloomington. For the next twenty years, she worked at slightly more interesting jobs and occasionally was even allowed to write some technical thing or another. She retired from drudgery in 2018 and moved to rural Oregon where she now takes long walks with her canine companion, Silly Lilly; and writes about political and social issues, and works on her own life stories.

More at katharinevalentino.medium.com

WATTS

Virginia Watts is the author of poetry and stories found in *CRAFT, The Florida Review, Two Thirds North, Pithead Chapel, Permafrost Magazine, Broadkill Review* and others. Her poetry chapbooks are available from Moonstone Press. She is a three-time Pushcart Prize and Best of the Net nominee. A short story collection is upcoming from Devil's Party Press.

More at virginiawatts.com

...to all a good night.